# I'm not leaving.

by Carl Wilkens

World Outside My Shoes
Spokane, WA

To order additional copies, please email us:
ImNotLeavingRwanda@gmail.com

Or you can order online:
www.ImNotLeavingRwanda.com

Printed in the United States of America
Editor, Brooke Schlange
Cover design by Bryan Gray
Cover photo by Sara Bäckman
Eight printing, 2018

The author takes full responsibility for the accuracy of the
information in this book. The views are his and the conversations
quoted here are either reconstructed from his memory or
taken from the tapes he made during the genocide. Some of
the names have been changed to protect individual privacy.

ISBN 978-1-4507-8080-3

# Dedicated

*To my Teresa Lynne*

*She didn't stand with me*

*I didn't stand with her*

*We stood together*

# Table of Contents

# Introduction

With a tragedy of such epic proportions as the 1994 Rwandan genocide against the Tutsi, with a complete shredding of a whole society, how could we ever hope to understand—even a bit—why it happened, how it happened, how it could have been prevented, and how it could have been stopped? I think our best hope of learning and gaining understanding begins in collecting as many witness, victim, and perpetrator accounts as possible, with each person sharing what they saw, what they experienced. This book is an attempt to give the world a look at various people living in Kigali during this extraordinarily brutal and violent time, a look through the eyes of a young American who was living there with his wife and small children—a look through my eyes.

While the stories written here happened during the genocide, this book is not really about genocide. It is more about the choices people made, actions people took, courage people showed, and sacrifices people gave in the face of genocide.

One of my hopes is that the stories contained here will help us each see something of ourselves in the people who survived this hundred-day calamity, and those who did not. Perhaps glimpses of things wanted in our own lives will be seen, as well as glimpses of things we most definitely do not want. My other hope is that these stories will connect in a way that will move each of us deeper in our commitment to end genocide.

I want to make it plain from the beginning that the stories in this book are completely inadequate to represent the horror and loss that happened during the genocide. It was so much worse than I could ever write and, as I have already said, that is not my purpose in writing.

When figures involving the loss of life begin to enter into the thousands and hundreds of thousands, they quickly become cold statistics that often blind us more than they inform us. But when we look at individual lives through stories, we find ourselves informed in ways that will stay with us and potentially make us more whole, more human.

Because this book does not communicate the enormous loss resulting from the genocide, and because I was there, I'm compelled here at the beginning to include, at minimum, the following look at the extermination of more than 800,000 lives. It is a brief look, and yes, I use statistics, but I attempt to use them in a different way than usual. Please take your time to articulate each digit and syllable, maybe even reading the following portion aloud, letting your ears hear the words echo off the walls wherever you are.

We lost:
- 18,465 gentle, never-a-harsh-word great-grandfathers
- 23,659 searching, wide-eyed infants
- 178,147 do-anything-for-their-families (I mean *anything*) moms
- 73,952 teasing, endlessly annoying gradeschool boys
- 19,320 quietly excited, wedding-planning brides
- 16,834 nearly blind, always encouraging grandmothers pulled from their beds
- 22,465 disciplined, ripped, eager athletes in training
- 21,872 always-quick-with-a-kind-word aunties
- 34,298 young men working hard to save up the bride price
- 25,359 patient, encouraging school teachers
- 39,293 girls at the age of a first crush
- 17,426 sons who spoke to their elders with respect
- 214,589 protective dads

I came to the point where I had to stop estimating numbers for the nurses, pastors, priests, artists, and craftsmen killed. It's too painful to continue coming up with more categories to list after the numbers. 48,398 *who?* 15,763 *who?* I simply cannot describe in words and numbers the catastrophic loss experienced by Rwanda and by our whole global community.

These estimates, these best guesses of mine, could be way off. My hope is to simply, or not-so-simply, walk with you around this statistical mountain of humans who were needlessly slaughtered and then stop. Stop and focus more closely *on the mountain* for a moment and then imagine the empty places and spaces no longer filled by these people in the lives of our neighbors in Rwanda.

Since 2004 I have been traveling around America, mostly to schools, sharing some of the stories in this book and speaking out against exclusive thinking that says, "My world would be better without you in it." I would like to end this introduction with a letter from a high school student who was taking a class on Facing History and Ourselves about genocide and the Holocaust. She sent it to me following a presentation I shared at her high school:

*Mr. Carl Wilkens,*

*So, our teacher tells us we're having a speaker come in to talk to us about the Rwandan genocide. So I'm like, #!\*@, way to put a damper on my day. Because, see, I really, really like this class, and maybe it's not exactly fun learning about how people tend to kill each other en masse, but I'm definitely glad to be taking the course.*

*So I'm taking this class for a reason, you know, but at the same time it's really hard to go from human rights atrocities to physics, or writing, or whatever I have next block—to learn about all this stuff and think about what it means to be human, and judgment, and values, and the legalities of slaughter, and then go work on integrals.*

*Sometimes it makes it hard to go around and do the school thing knowing that there are people dying out there—we're having a speaker, and if just reading about this stuff has been hard, what's a real live speaker going to be like? What if I have a calculus test the next block? So, I wasn't exactly dreading your visit, but I was definitely a bit, uh, apprehensive.*

*And then you show up, and you start talking, and you're funny, really funny, and everyone's sitting there wondering if we're allowed to laugh at the genocide speaker. And you answered that for us, yes, yes, you have to laugh, you have to look for a bright side. Instead of having a bunch of weeping, depressed teens, you left us a group of hopeful people. I didn't expect that.*

*So often we are taught this material by shock value, by descriptions of horrors and atrocities, and we need to see that, to learn that, because it's the truth—but then we also need to hear that really, people can do nice things for each other, even in the middle of those horrors.*

*So thank you, for flying across the country to tell us what we were all supposed to learn in kindergarten but never really figured out— people are decent, start small, do what you think is right, what you think is kind.*

*It makes a difference to hear it from someone who has been there, seen things none of us can ever imagine, and still comes to talk to a bunch of teenagers and tell us to play nice with each other. Kind of restores my faith in humanity.*

*Your visit was very much appreciated.*

*G—Lexington High School Junior*

Courage, as you travel through these stories. In our traveling to schools we have seen again and again the power stories have to change the way we think, which impacts the way we feel, which often changes the way we act. Or to put it another way - Sustainable change in feelings and actions comes through changed thinking: Thinking > Feelings > Actions ☺

Peace, Carl

Please send comments to ImNotLeavingRwanda@gmail.com

# Map of Kigali

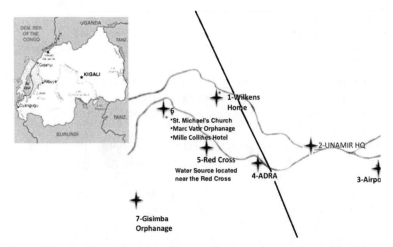

The solid line cutting Kigali in half shows the boundary on the left held by government forces and on the right controlled by rebel forces.

## List of Characters Mentioned More Than Once

**Aaron:** Religious book translator
**Angelique:** Food distribution volunteer, wounded neighbor
**Anitha:** Young lady who lived and worked in our home for the three years prior to the genocide—ID card read "Tutsi"
**Bernard:** Helper of the courtyard people hiding in the middle of Kigali
**Damas Gisimba:** Director of Gisimba Orphanage
**Dassan:** ADRA colleague who worked with me during genocide
**Edith:** My mother
**Father Wenceslas Munyeshyaka:** Priest at the Holy Family Church
**Jean-Francois:** Brother of Damas, the Gisimba Orphanage director
**Kambanda:** Genocidal prime minister
**Gasigwa:** ADRA colleague who worked with me during genocide
**General Dallaire:** Force Commander of UNAMIR
**Heri:** Ran the orphanage down the street from our home
**Janvier:** Our young night watchman—ID card read "Tutsi"
**James:** Expatriate Red Cross doctor who did a rotation in Kigali
**John:** My father
**Lisa:** Our middle child, age 7 at the time
**Major Emmanuel:** Rescued the Nyamirambo Church people
**Major Rose Kabuye:** RPF-appointed Mayor of Kigali
**Mambo:** In charge of the Ministry of Transportation garage
**Marc Vaiter:** Frenchman who remained in Kigali with his orphans
**Mindy:** Our firstborn, age 10 at the time
**Mitch Scoggins:** Nairobi friend, worked at ADRA/South Sudan office
**Mama Papa Zero:** UNAMIR humanitarian team
**Mrs. Seraya (Foibe):** The wife of Pastor Seraya, stayed in our home
**Pastor Seraya:** Rwanda Union Mission treasurer, stayed in our home
**Patrick:** The logistics man at the International Committee for the Red Cross (ICRC)
**Philippe Gaillard:** Chief of International Committee for the Red Cross
**Shaun:** Our youngest child, age 5 at the time
**Simeon:** ADRA accountant
**Teresa:** My wife
**Tharcisse Renzaho:** Military colonel, prefect (governor) for Kigali, appointed during the genocide
**Thomas:** ADRA colleague
**Triphine:** Medical person at Gisimba Orphanage
**Wayne Ulrich:** Doctors Without Borders (MSF) logistics man

# Chapter 1
# **Why Stay**

The white United Nations tank idled loudly outside the gates of our home as I hugged and kissed my parents and our three children–Mindy, Lisa, and Shaun–goodbye. Holding Teresa, my wife, extra tight, I whispered, "Two weeks maximum, Love. This thing can't last more than two weeks, then I'll come see you and the kids in Burundi, and probably in three weeks it'll be okay for you to come home. I love you!"

Taking my hand, Teresa stepped up into our pickup camper. I slowly closed the door behind her, pushing until I heard the latch click, and then I headed down the driveway. As I opened the gate, Colonel Luc Marchal, the commander of the Belgian troops in the UN force, emerged from the tank manhole and jumped down to my level. While shaking his hand, I couldn't thank him enough for escorting my family to the evacuation assembly-point at the U.S. ambassador's home. The Colonel didn't want to leave Rwanda, this picturesque little jewel on the belly button of Africa, until he felt he had done everything possible to complete his mission of evacuating all the foreigners.

His men formed a circle around the perimeter of the tank with their rifles at the ready as our pickup camper crept down the driveway and poked its nose out onto the dirt road. The Belgian soldiers quickly piled back into the tank and led the way. Less than a hundred meters down the road stood a barrier, nothing but a log that was raised up on two stones to indicate an ID checkpoint. Those manning the barrier scattered as the tank approached. I watched Colonel Marchal once again climb out of his military machine and pitch the log aside. He could easily have driven over it, but our pickup couldn't have.

Dad was at the wheel, sticking to the backside of that tank like a magnet. When they got to the intersection, the tank couldn't make the right-hand turn in one swing. It started to roll back to make a second cut. Dad searched for reverse as the track of the tank crushed his parking light. At the last moment he popped the pickup camper into gear and lurched backwards.

I stood barefoot in the middle of our dusty street, waving goodbye to the most precious people in the world. The "Armadillo"—that's what we called our camper—waddled around the corner as I lowered my hand. Looking around, I made sure our neighbors saw that I was not leaving. If anyone had ideas about breaking into our home and going after Anitha, the young lady who worked for us, or Janvier, our young night watchman, I would be there. I didn't know what I would do if we were attacked, but I would be there. Going back inside our home, I could see the fear on the faces of Anitha and Janvier. Their ID cards both had the word *Tutsi* on them, classifying them among Rwanda's minority tribe. But now it was more than simply a tribal designation—it marked them for extermination.

For Teresa and me, Anitha and Janvier put a very real face on the Tutsi people of Rwanda. Having them physically with us in our home kept our hearts engaged in our decision for me to stay, preventing logic or fear from dominating our thoughts. It's amazing how the physical presence of a person can change the outcome of a situation. Simply *being there* is often the most powerful factor in making the right decision—a decision we will not regret for the rest of our lives.

Anitha and Janvier's presence impacted our thinking, keeping me in Rwanda. Now I counted on my presence to impact the thinking of the killers and keep them away from us.

## Plane Crash

Four years earlier, in March 1990, Teresa and I had come to Rwanda with our three children, ages 6, 3, and 1½ years at that time. I was the country director of ADRA, the humanitarian arm of the Seventh-day Adventist Church.

Dad came to Kigali in January 1994 to manage the financial

side of a post-war[1] clinic rehab project, and Mom had come for the last three weeks of his stay. They were both scheduled to return home to the States in five days.

At exactly 6 p.m. on April 6, 1994, the lights went out on us at the Adventist Development and Relief Agency (ADRA) offices in Kigali. Losing electricity didn't surprise me. In the light of the setting sun I called out to Mom and Dad, "Let's call it a day and head home. If the electricity's off here, it might be off at home, and I'm pretty sure Lisa and Shaun are alone with Anitha. Teresa was planning on taking Mindy to visit a friend at another missionary's home."

The lights were on as we pulled up to the house—a good sign. Electricity had been pretty sketchy in the evenings recently. After dinner, everyone was busy doing his or her own thing when we heard a louder-than-normal explosion. I say "louder-than-normal" because grenade explosions around the city had become rather commonplace.

The international community had forced "democracy" on Rwanda. Both the World Bank and the International Monetary Fund had refused to support a one-party state any longer. Overnight, more than a dozen political parties sprang up. The arrival of this "democracy" brought instability that expressed itself with increasing levels of petty and sometimes not-so-petty crime. Some people now acted as if they were entitled to do whatever they pleased.

"That was a loud one," Dad said.

"Yeah," I replied. "I wonder if it was an ammunition stockpile or something."

We didn't think much more about it until the phone rang twenty minutes later. Jake, a Canadian friend teaching at the Adventist University located in the northwest corner of the country, anxiously asked, "Can you see the flames?"

"What flames?" I asked.

"They're announcing on the radio that the president's plane

---

[1] There was a three-year civil war in Rwanda from 1990 to 1993 before the genocide.

was shot down as it was landing!" he announced somewhat disbelievingly.

"Wow, we did hear a loud explosion. I'll go outside and look towards the airport." Hanging up the phone, I turned to my family. "The president's plane was just shot down!"

A stunned silence filled the room, freezing everyone in place. The kids' faces mirrored the question marks on the adult faces. I went outside but couldn't see any flames glowing in the starry sky because of the hills between us and the airport five miles away.

A few minutes later we heard the first of sporadic gunfire echo through the hills and valleys of our city. Teresa and I telephoned other missionary families to see how they were. Teresa remembers one call in particular with Betty Stanic, a volunteer from the former Yugoslavia. Betty had been talking with some of her Belgian UN peacekeeper friends, and she ended the conversation by saying, "I'm scared." Her comment caught Teresa off guard. We had been living with this tension for so long that we did not immediately recognize how the president's plane crash had spiked the situation to a very dangerous level.

Still, not feeling threatened, we all went to sleep in our own beds that night, unaware of the plans that had been set in motion by the president's assassination—plans that would separate this tiny nation, like a single train car, from the rest of the planet and send it plunging into the most tragic one hundred days of the twentieth century.

## Chapter 2
# Warning Signs

A few weeks prior to the plane crash, I called a meeting with the other American Adventist missionaries in Kigali. I felt it was important to talk about what we would do if fighting between the government forces and the Rwandan Patriotic Front (RPF)[2] broke out again.

I had been selected as the liaison between the U.S. embassy and this group of missionaries, which meant attending regular security briefings at the embassy. The most recent briefing included discussions about evacuation plans and procedures. Assembly points had been identified around Kigali should it become necessary to flee. I remember ending the meeting with the missionaries by saying that if evacuation plans were implemented, it would be up to each family to decide what was best for them and that they would not be pressured to stay or go.

Although war had been going on for the past three years, the capital city of Kigali had remained relatively untouched physically, and life went on as usual. That calm was now rapidly disintegrating. Rumors spread throughout the city of pickup trucks arriving in the night, loaded with weapons, which were being stashed around town. In response to the recent violent demonstrations, the government enforced 24-hour curfews from time to time. Murders of opposition party leaders and Tutsis were becoming more numerous.

In December 1993, political members of the RPF movement

---

[2] The RPF was composed of Rwandan exiles, mostly of Tutsi origin, who had fled attacks in 1959. These exiles had expected to return home once things settled down, but the Rwandan government resisted their return for years, and finally these Tutsi people picked up guns and invaded Rwanda in October of 1990, marking the beginning of a civil war that lasted 3 years. The RPF's disciplined and determined fighting eventually forced the Rwandan government to the negotiating table, and in August 1993, the Broad Based Transitional Government (BBTG) was hammered out. The proposed government included members from the different parties in Rwanda as well as the RPF and would rule until elections were held.

had arrived in Kigali for the installation of the Broad Based Transitional Government (BBTG). Along with them came 600 RPF soldiers to ensure their safety. They were all housed in the Parliament building, and their presence added much to the growing level of unease for some, but others took it as a sign that peace really was coming to Rwanda.

The BBTG was seen as the key to building lasting peace in Rwanda. Rwandans and foreigners alike were counting on the BBTG to defuse what was beginning to feel like a ticking time bomb. With the continuing delays in installing it, the horizon was growing darker and darker.

In the fall of 1993, the UN sent the United Nations Assistance Mission in Rwanda (UNAMIR) to monitor and facilitate the launch of the BBTG. Their highly visible and growing presence during the months before the president's assassination gave us the sense that they were becoming a permanent part of the landscape. We used to say you couldn't spit in Kigali without hitting a vehicle branded by the bold black UN letters. In the weeks preceding April 6, UNAMIR troops started patrolling the streets on foot in an effort to calm the mounting tensions. Seeing squads of Belgian soldiers—eight men strong, wearing the blue UN beret and full military uniform with assault rifles, helmets, and radio antennas wobbling in the air with every step—caused people to fall into a false sense of security.

This false sense of security contributed greatly to the enormous losses that were soon to be experienced. For the foreign community these losses were minimal in contrast to what the Rwandan community lost. When deaths start to number in the hundreds of thousands, the numbers quickly turn to cold statistics. But if we divide those statistics between different groups of people,[3] maybe we can begin to grasp in a very small way the enormous loss of life experienced by the Rwandan community and all of us on this planet.

I suspect that if UNAMIR had not come across as protectors, many Rwandans would have taken necessary precautions to

[3] See introduction to the book.

safeguard themselves and their families. Many would probably have fled toward the borders when they saw the warning signs and heard the RTLM[4] radio station blasting across Rwanda its hate radio— full of hate musicians, hate comedians, and hate speech makers.

Committing genocide is hard work; it takes a lot of planning and preparation. I've often wondered how many genocides have been attempted and failed. Looking back in Rwanda, it is easy to see how the actions of the UNAMIR soldiers were used by the genocide planners to make their vicious work easier. Easier, not only because of the false sense of security the UN portrayed, which encouraged people not to flee, but also because UNAMIR's presence was used to facilitate the logistical work of killing.

During the first week of the genocide, thousands of people fled to UNAMIR camps for protection. When the UNAMIR forces withdrew, the Interahamwe[5] closed in on all of those innocent families conveniently gathered in well-marked locations around Kigali and the rest of the country. Instead of needing to go from house to house searching in closets, under beds, in the ceilings, or out in the banana plantations for many of the Tutsi and moderate Hutu families, the Interahamwe need only go from UNAMIR camp to UNAMIR camp. Their killing was made so much easier, and the betrayed families of Rwanda were slaughtered right where UNAMIR, under very clear orders, had abandoned them.

---

[4] RTLM (Radio-Télévision Libre des Milles Collines or Thousand Hills Free Radio & Television) was the radio station which broadcast propaganda against the Tutsi, moderate Hutu, UNAMIR, and Belgians from July 8, 1993, to July 31, 1994. It played a key role in preparing for the genocide and then in executing the genocide. Its contemporary DJs and music made it very popular among the youth, many of whom later became Interahamwe. I don't think the genocide could have been carried out as effectively as it was without RTLM.

[5] *Interahamwe* is a Kinyarwanda word that means "those who work or stand together." It is the term now used for the killing squads that were trained in preparation for the genocide. It is significant to note that before the genocide only one in ten students could get into secondary school because there were not enough schools. These students who could not go on in their education provided a fertile pool for genocide planners to recruit from.

Chapter 3

# Memories From the First Day

What do I remember about that Thursday, the day after the plane crash?

I remember bullets and machine-gun fire, both in our own neighborhood and from across the valley toward the center of town. I remember the American embassy sending out word that there would be no evacuation. U.S. intelligence sources indicated that the RPF would take over the city in less than four days, and it would be more dangerous to try to evacuate than to stay in our homes and keep our heads down.

I remember spending much time on the HF (high frequency) communication radio we had in our home. This radio was normally used to facilitate the development work we were involved in. That Thursday, I was compiling a list of nationalities and passport numbers for the Adventist expatriates scattered around Rwanda. We had missionaries from Belgium, France, Denmark, Brazil, Spain, Canada, Australia, Madagascar, Sri Lanka, and the United States.

I remember thinking up ways, along with Teresa, to distract our children from the gunfire, shouting, and crashing sounds as homes in our own neighborhood were invaded and looted, and families slaughtered. I told our kids that we were going to learn a new game, and it started with all of us lying down together near the front door. Our goal was to reach the other end of the house, but any time we heard a gunshot, if a person's stomach was not touching the floor, that person had to go back and start over. It didn't seem possible that we were playing games in our house while, in homes nearby, parents watched helplessly as their children were hacked and bludgeoned to death in front of them.

I remember learning that much of the pounding and gunfire was coming from a beautiful three-story home, several doors down from us. The father was a banker, and because of his influential position and the fact that his ID card said "Tutsi," they were at the top of the local list to be killed.

Neighbors later said that the mother and father had boosted their two youngest children over the fence into the yard of the orphanage next door, hoping they might be spared, and that their teenage son had burrowed into a pile of brush in the back yard. The children survived, but the mother and father did not. Their hiding place, a small closet under the stairway, kept them safe for an hour or so, while the house was being looted.

For reasons I have yet to understand, torture nearly always preceded death, and their murders were no different. Neighbors later told us how the mother's broken body had been draped over the fence in their front yard. During a lull in the chaos, I peeked out of our window and saw their furniture and appliances being marched down the street on the heads and backs of their killers.

### Gakoni Orphanage

There is one radio conversation, still clear in my mind, that I know I will never forget. I was talking with a volunteer at Gakoni Orphanage, which was about a two-and-a-half-hour drive to the east of us. The static on the airwaves was making communication very difficult, and I was barely able to make out their desperate plea for help:

*"Please try to contact the UN and send help! More than a hundred people have come into our front yard looking for protection, and someone is being HACKED TO DEATH RIGHT NOW, outside my window! Please help us! Do you copy?"*

Teresa and I, along with Mom and Dad, were all gathered around the radio, stunned, frozen in place, while I speechlessly held the microphone in my hand. At that moment, I looked over and saw Mindy standing in the doorway, listening to this horror play out over the airwaves. Her large brown eyes were full of concern and confusion, and I said, "Teresa, take her—please take her away."

After repeated dialing and busy signals, I managed to raise

someone at the UN headquarters office in Kigali. I asked if they had soldiers anywhere near Gakoni Orphanage in Commune Murambi. The UN soldier sounded rattled, and what he told me next explained why.

He exclaimed, "We lost the airport!"

I was shocked. "What do you mean, 'lost the airport'?" I asked.

"We're cut off and don't have access to the airport because of the fighting," he explained.

That's when I began to realize how wrong we were in believing for the last three months that the UN could provide security. The soldier gave me phone numbers to the UN contingent in Byumba, who, under normal circumstances, would have been about 90 minutes from the orphanage. When I finally got through to Byumba, Colonel Yachee from Ghana gave me a sliver of hope. He grasped the severity of the situation quickly and said he would do his best to send men to the orphanage. I relayed this bit of promising information back to the retired American and Australian volunteers at the orphanage. Amazingly, two UN soldiers eventually reached the orphanage that day. Their heroic and life-risking efforts during this dangerous time are just a small example of the heart and courage that so many UNAMIR soldiers displayed.

That afternoon we contacted MSF,[6] a humanitarian group who were evacuating foreign staff from their outpost not far from the orphanage. They agreed to stop and collect the orphanage volunteers, who by this time had all decided to leave, and eventually they all fled to Tanzania.

The next day, government officials came to the orphanage with trucks and removed the families seeking refuge.

They murdered nearly all of them in this growing tsunami, this horrible man-made disaster. The term *genocide* began circulating through the international media before April ended.

When the genocide ended in Kigali three months later, I drove the two-and-a-half hours to Gakoni Orphanage and was amazed

---

[6] Médecins Sans Frontières or Doctors Without Borders

at what I saw when I walked onto the campus: chickens pecked peacefully among the flower beds and clean laundry waved from the clothesline. The Rwandans working there said it was only a matter of weeks (very, very long weeks) from when the genocide started to the time the RPF secured the area and stopped the killings. The orphanage workers said the RPF had been supplying them with rice and other goods, and not one of the orphans had been harmed.

Chapter 4

# Their Kids Play With Our Kids

**Neighbors Between the Machetes and Us**

Friday morning Anitha came in from the back yard with an unbelievable story. She had been talking with our neighbors through the fence, and they told her the Interahamwe had come to our gate the previous night, armed with machetes, clubs, and assault rifles. When our neighbors found out the militia were gathering at our gate, they came and stood between this gang of killers and our family. It was hard to take in what Anitha was telling us because even though we had heard the gunfire around our neighborhood, we hadn't realized *our* home had been targeted.

We asked Anitha how our neighbors had managed to turn the killers away, and she said our neighbors first told the Interahamwe that we were not Belgian (there had been rumors flying around that the Belgians had shot down the president's plane). They also told them that we had been living here for several years and recounted some of our small acts of kindness, like taking people to the hospital in the middle of the night.

Of all the stories told to the Interahamwe that night, one thing stood out above the rest. Anitha explained that our neighbors told the killers, *This family's children play with our children.*

Mindy, Lisa, and Shaun had spent four years growing up with the Rwandan kids in our community—playing, learning, and building bonds together.

**I have no doubt the relationships our children built in our neighborhood were the single most important factor that inspired and moved our neighbors to stand up for us that night.**

It is not an exaggeration to say that our family easily could have been killed during those dark hours. At a minimum, we would have been terrorized and robbed. Years later, when I was able to sit down and talk to our neighbors about those events and try again to communicate our gratitude to them, I said, "We could easily have been killed that night." Without hesitation they simply replied, "Yes."

Our family's story could have ended that Thursday night, April 7, along with the stories of so many Rwandan families who lost their lives, but we are alive today because mothers, aunts, and grandmas stood up for us. And to think they were armed only with stories.

### 72-hour Cease-Fire

Friday morning we received a fax from my oldest brother, Barry, in Phoenix, Arizona. He was checking up on us; the fax arrived just minutes before the phone lines in our neighborhood went out for good. We were now cut off from communication with family in the States. However, despite the lack of telephone communication, we did manage to keep radio contact with the embassy and other mission stations around the country.

That same day the U.S. embassy told us the fighting was not going to end as quickly as they thought; evacuations were beginning the next day and ending Sunday. A 72-hour cease-fire had been brokered between the RPF and a new Rwandan government.[7] This cease-fire provided a window of opportunity for foreigners living in Rwanda to get out. Although most European governments were flying their citizens out, we were told by the embassy there was too

---

[7] With the president dead, soldiers went to the prime minister's home and killed her. The planners of the genocide then put their own government in place.

much risk of the planes coming under fire and that driving would be a safer option. German and Canadian citizens also joined the American road convoy. When I learned that Kigali's sizable Indian population was also leaving, I remember thinking, *This must be a whole lot worse than anything we've had up to this point.* The Indian community, made up mostly of families permanently settled in Rwanda, normally weathered whatever storm came along.

Our Kigali Adventist group decided to join the Sunday morning convoy, and so we began preparations to drive out to Burundi. The thought of my staying, with Teresa and the children leaving, was not a new idea. There had been evacuation talk in October 1990 at the beginning of the civil war. While some expatriates left, Teresa and I decided after careful discussions to remain in the country with our children.

In the weeks preceding the genocide, when the U.S. embassy started making plans for a possible evacuation, Teresa and I talked again about our options and decided that if evacuation became necessary this time, she and the kids would leave and I would stay. Of course, talking about it and actually doing it can be two very different things.

During that Friday afternoon packing session, Teresa and I decided to bring out the Christmas and birthday presents we had purchased on our last furlough to the States. The kids were excited, and it was a welcome distraction for us all. Watching our children excitedly open their presents and packages, as they would have on Christmas morning, filled us both with a strange mixture of joy and sorrow. Dwelling on the fact that these could be the last hours I would ever have with my family was something I did not allow myself to do at the time, but I have thought about it a lot since.

Sitting at the radio Friday evening, I tuned to the restricted frequency our embassy used. Unashamedly, I eavesdropped on a conversation between our embassy in Kigali and the American embassy in Nairobi, Kenya. They were talking about shredding documents and other procedures that the Kigali embassy was supposed to be executing.

A mysterious interlude occurred when somebody called "Movie Star" came on the frequency and tried to establish communication with the Kigali embassy operator. The embassy radio operator asked for identification details, but "Movie Star" refused to give any. Then the embassy operator said, "We don't know any 'Movie Star.' Get off this frequency. This channel is for official business only." "Movie Star" eventually did fall silent.

Later that evening I tuned in again and heard "Movie Star" talking to a more relaxed embassy operator and thought, *That's strange.* Only much later did I learn that "Movie Star" was the radio name for the group of 300 U.S. Marines who had landed in Bujumbura, Burundi. They were on standby to assist in the evacuation of Americans if necessary.

I was surprised when George Moose, the Assistant Secretary of State for African Affairs, came over the airwaves from Washington, D.C., via a radiophone patch. While listening at different points throughout the evening to the various conversations, it slowly began to dawn on me that the Kigali embassy was going to be closed down completely. I was amazed how fast events were unfolding. I had always expected that if things got really bad, the embassy would reduce to a minimal staff, including the ambassador and a few key personnel. Subconsciously I think that's what I still expected. Suddenly it became crystal clear: *everybody was leaving!*

## I'm Not Leaving

Saturday morning Teresa and I told Mom and Dad that I would be staying in Kigali. The night before, we had put the kids to bed in the hallway, and after they were asleep we quietly went into our bedroom to talk and pray about our decision. I don't remember details from that conversation. For anyone looking at this story from the outside it would seem that this was such a pivotal point— deciding whether to stay or not. Yet as Teresa and I talked, it was just so very obvious to both of us that there was no way we would abandon Janvier and Anitha with their Tutsi ID cards to fend for themselves.

Janvier had recently been hired to work as the night watchman at our home. His dad was a warm friend of our family, having worked in and around our home in times past. Anitha had lived and worked in our home doing housekeeping for the past three years. With a gentle smile, she would put up with or sometimes even join in the kids' antics. It was clear from the way she interacted with them that she honestly treasured each one and contributed any way she could in their development. There was never a harsh or impatient word from Anitha. Very close bonds had been created, probably closer than any of us really understood at that time. We had no doubt that if we left, Janvier and Anitha would be killed.

That is exactly what happened to so many individuals and families in Rwanda who were seeking refuge in the homes, schools, churches, and hospitals where foreigners were present—they were slaughtered. This is not to say that the presence of foreigners was a guarantee of safety for Rwandans. As it turned out, so many Rwandans were killed in those first days before the evacuation. They were killed in spite of the fact that foreigners were right there begging the killers to stop. I write about this not to condemn anyone who left or to say that there were any obvious easy answers during this time. There were no easy answers.

In the end three factors keep coming to the top of my list of reasons for staying. First, the embassy had made it clear that Rwandans could not be evacuated in our vehicles and it was out f the question to consider leaving Anitha and Janvier to face an almost certain death alone. Second, Teresa was totally with me on the decision. This was huge. She never once said, "what about me and the children. And finally, our relationship with our Maker gave us conviction, strength, and hope to do what we were convinced was right.

I also want to mention one incredible realization that struck me as I reflected on our decision for me to stay: neither Janvier nor Anitha ever once asked me to stay. Not once did they ask me to put my life on the line for them.

To say that Mom and Dad were initially not at all open to our plan would be an understatement. Even though it was *their* life example and the things *they* had taught us boys that significantly impacted my decision to stay, they were having serious trouble letting go. I wish I could remember more details of the conversation that followed our announcement that I was staying, but I can't. I've often wondered what I would have done if I'd been in Dad's shoes. I'm so grateful that I wasn't. In the end, when Dad saw how determined Teresa and I were, he said, "OK, Carl. If you're staying, I'm staying."

"No, Dad," I replied. "I need you to take Teresa and the kids out."

It wasn't that Teresa couldn't have done it herself, but I felt a whole lot better knowing that Dad would be with them.

That afternoon Teresa baked a batch of cookies for the kids. During what could have been our last ever evening together, we sat on our front porch and watched as buses came down the hill from the center of town, ferrying tourists from hotels to the airport. As I watched those buses and lines of cars leaving, I thought to myself, *If the people of Rwanda ever needed help, NOW IS THE TIME. Instead, everybody is leaving.*

Later that evening we stashed our electronics and other valuables up in the ceiling, fully expecting that our home would be looted before this was all over.

Sunday morning is blurry in my memory. I do remember helping Teresa gather and pack last-minute things for the family. Mom had been crying, and I don't think she slept at all the night before. Dad was silently lending a hand where he could. This wasn't the first time I had seen him move about with that calm, controlled exterior, while things on the inside were undoubtedly anything but calm. I knew beyond a shadow of a doubt that I could count on him to take my family to safety, but I also knew we still didn't see eye-to-eye on the decision Teresa and I had made for me to stay.

There were several radio conversations that morning as I helped coordinate the evacuation of other missionaries. Despite being in the middle of a 72-hour cease-fire, the sound of gunfire still echoed through the hills.

The embassy had instructed us to tie white t-shirts to our vehicles' radio antennas and head to the nearest evacuation assembly point. Driving out into the bedlam with only a white t-shirt flapping in the breeze for protection didn't sound very reassuring to me. Fortunately, the journey was made safer thanks to Betty Stanic, the volunteer from the former Yugoslavia. Two days earlier Betty had asked friends among the Belgian UNAMIR soldiers to bring her to our house, and now we made radio contact with these soldiers. They agreed to send a UNAMIR tank to escort our family to the U.S. ambassador's home, our closest designated assembly point.

At 10 a.m., minutes before the tank arrived, I had the following radio conversation with Laura Lane, our U.S. consulate officer:

**Carl:** *The missionaries at the dental compound are making their way to the ambassador's home. Over.*

**Laura:** *Good copy. Over.*

**Carl:** *I'm ready to send my family to the ambassador's home now. Over.*

**Laura:** *What do you mean "send" your family? Over.*

**Carl:** *I'm not leaving. Over.*

**Laura:** *We are all leaving. You don't have a choice. Over.*

**Carl:** *As a private American citizen, I do have a choice. I'm not leaving. Over.*

**Laura:** *OK. Well, then . . . then you need to sign a paper stating that you have refused the help of the United States government to leave Rwanda. Over.*

**Carl:** *OK. Over.*

I took one of Mindy's school notebooks, found a blank page, and wrote with a pencil, *"I have refused the help of the United States government to leave Rwanda."* I signed and dated the declaration, tore the page from its spiral binding, folded it, and handed it to Teresa. This is an event that has engraved itself permanently into my memory. To some it might seem melodramatic, but you have to understand that up to this point I had this pride and trust in America. Signing, dating, and folding this paper did not take long, but it caused me to pause and think deeply about what that pride and trust really meant. Cutting ties with possible assistance from the U.S. government was not something I was taking lightly. Looking back, I think this was the beginning of a shift from trusting in institutions and governments to trusting in individuals.

As for Laura Lane, she was and still is a wonderful friend. We all knew we were doing what we each had to do; she would have stayed in Rwanda too if she hadn't had the responsibility of getting all the Americans out. I found out later she tried to convince the State Department to let her and other embassy staff set up a safe haven at the U.S. embassy. When that was not allowed, she did everything she could to help the people of Rwanda. She issued "fiancé visas" to some and hid others, both Hutu and Tutsi, in the trunks of vehicles that were part of the last convoy, which she and her husband, Greg, shepherded out of Rwanda. She stayed in touch with Teresa in Nairobi throughout the genocide and on several occasions told her, "You just say the word, and one way or another, we'll go get Carl!" Laura did an incredible job.[8]

As I said goodbye to Teresa and the children, we tried very hard to focus on what had to be done and the practical aspects of their departure. Looking back it seems as if we had an unspoken agreement not to mention worries or fears. We tried to keep it positive, to keep it light. Neither one of us wanted to put words to the thought that this could very well be our last goodbye.

---

[8] Read more about Laura Lane's role at: http://www.pbs.org/wgbh/pages/frontline/shows/ghosts/interviews/lane.html

## Chapter 5

# Convoy Out

As I watched our camper disappear around the corner, tight on the tank's tail, an incredibly helpless feeling came over me. The realization that there was nothing, absolutely nothing, I could do to protect my family was unnerving, to say the least. When Teresa made radio contact from the ambassador's home, saying they arrived there safely less than an hour later, I let out a long deep breath and thought, *OK, that's one leg of the journey down.*

All the other missionaries from the dental compound and neighborhood had also arrived without incident. Ranjan, one of the dentists, was surprised I wasn't there and said incredulously to Teresa, "I didn't know we could stay!"

Through the years I've often wondered how many other people "didn't know they could stay." On one hand, the most natural and smart thing to do is to get out when killing is happening all around. We often don't even think that we might have another choice. And there are times when the actions of others may greatly limit our choices, but they can never completely take them away. When I think about choices, I think about what Holocaust survivor and author Viktor Frankl wrote in his book *Man's Search for Meaning:*

> We who lived in concentration camps can remember the men who walked through the huts comforting others, giving away their last piece of bread. They may have been few in number, but they offer sufficient proof that everything can be taken from a man but one thing: the last of the human freedoms—to choose one's attitude in any given set of circumstances, to choose one's own way. (2006 ed., p. 65, 66)

## Our Team Comes Together

About two hours later Teresa radioed me again to say that Pastor Seraya was on his way to our home. The pastor was the Rwanda Union Mission treasurer and was responsible for the finances of the 300,000-member Adventist church in Rwanda. Though "Hutu" was marked on the pastor's and his wife's ID cards, they were at risk from both the crossfire and the fact they could easily be labeled traitors for not joining the genocidal wave crashing down all over the country.

For the safety of evacuating Americans, our embassy had made it clear that no Rwandans would be allowed in the convoys. Earlier that morning I received a message from the Mathesons, who lived across the street from Pastor Seraya. They were wondering how they could help him and his wife.

"Tell the pastor and his wife to come to my house! I'm not leaving," I responded. So Pastor Seraya piggybacked on the missionary convoy to the American ambassador's home and then drove the final mile to our home alone. I gladly swung the gates open and welcomed them in. They had their nephew and his very pregnant wife in the back seat.[9]

Little did I know what key roles the pastor and his wife would play in maintaining the safety of the small team that was coming

---

[9] Several weeks later when the government relaxed the 24/7 curfews that followed the exodus of the foreigners, this young man took his expectant wife to calmer regions of the country.

together at our home, a team that was assembling itself in a rather haphazard fashion. The roles Pastor Seraya and his wife played, not only in our survival but also in the survival of so many others, cannot be overestimated and will probably never be fully known.

In those early days it wasn't just foreigners, Tutsis, and moderate Hutus who were fleeing Kigali. The violent military battle between the RPF and the government forces sent everybody running. If you were fortunate and had enough money, you hired a soldier or an Interahamwe with a weapon, packed your loved ones along with the "hired gun" in a car, and raced away as fast as you could.

I was so very grateful that Pastor and Mrs. Seraya chose not to flee but to come stay with me instead. Numerous times Mrs. Seraya was the first one to deal with the Interahamwe, whether to answer their questions about what was going on in our house or to buy food and supplies from them. Additionally, Pastor Seraya was not only a sounding board, giving insightful counsel throughout the three months we were together, but a provider of so many valuable plans and strategies. I loved his creative, yet sound, approach to the many problems we faced. Looking back, I cannot imagine going through the genocide without the wisdom, courage, and support of both of them.

Photo by Jackie Crombie Stonas

## Out at Last

With such unprecedented levels of killing taking place, it was a miracle that the American evacuation was as successful as it was.[10] Teresa's convoy reached Burundi, the country directly south of Rwanda, on Sunday evening, April 10.

Dad remembers one roadblock still in Kigali where a boy he estimated to be about twelve years old stuck a grenade threateningly through the window in his face. At another intersection, he had to stop to let a truck piled high with people, eyes wide open but their lives already lost, roll past. The lifeless cargo softly rose and fell as the vehicle lumbered through the potholes of Kigali's streets. Teresa, Mom, and the children were shielded in the camper from the inhuman sights that permanently fixed themselves in Dad's mind, as well as in the minds of everyone else who saw them.

Fortunately, the camper did a pretty good job of protecting our family from the chaos happening all around. Often, when the

---

[10] The embassy chose not to call in the Marines for assistance in the evacuation, believing that they had a better chance of getting the Americans out safely by not "militarizing" the operation. As it turned out, they were successful in talking down tense situations at roadblocks when the Interahamwe wanted to detain and search the convoy vehicles.

convoy was stopped at a roadblock, Interahamwe would bang on the sides of the camper and rock it back and forth. Teresa remembers hearing people trying to open the door handle several times and was so grateful that the lock held. The banging and rocking was frightening enough, but definitely milder than what was happening outside.

After a safe arrival in Burundi, my parents flew home to Spokane, Washington, while Teresa and the children, hoping to return to Rwanda soon, remained in the home of the ADRA/Burundi director, Bent Nielsen, and his wife, Evelyn. Ten days later, due to growing instability in Burundi, the American embassy advised all Americans to leave the country as soon as they were able.

Wanting to keep the children safe but not wanting to go any farther from our home in Rwanda than she had to, Teresa and the kids flew to Nairobi, Kenya, where the Lewises, another missionary family, graciously received them. I'm extremely grateful to friends like the Nielsen and Lewis families for their generous support of our family. A week later, toward the end of April, Teresa and the children were able to move into a church guest room near the center of Nairobi, where Teresa could have easier access to radio communication with me.

### Teresa in Nairobi

Had you been in Nairobi during the last half of April and into May of 1994, you might very well have seen my courageous, young wife walking through the bustling, crime-ridden streets. She would have been either on her way to or coming from downtown Nairobi, where she talked with me daily on whatever radio equipment she was able to locate. Every day, she would find someone to stay with the children and then walk or find a ride to either the ADRA/South Sudan office or the U.S. embassy in search of a radio for our conversations—conversations that were a real lifeline for me. In fact, we were able to talk every single day of the genocide except one.

Wayne, our ever-resourceful Doctors Without Borders friend, was sometimes able to send a driver to take Teresa to the embassy. After the first six weeks he somehow managed to have a radio installed in the apartment my family eventually moved into. It was so good to be able to talk directly with each of the children. In addition to Wayne's kindness, one of his colleagues, Juliana Voicu, became a close friend. Her quiet and consistent support meant so much to Teresa. Then for the final weeks of the genocide, Barb Anderson, a gracious and fun-loving family friend, came from Spokane, Washington, to stay with Teresa and the children. Her can-do spirit brought much joy and encouragement, brightening every place she went.

Another supportive friend during these stressful times was Mitch Scoggins, who worked at the ADRA/South Sudan office and met Teresa and the kids at the airport when they first arrived in Nairobi. He took them in one of those big, black British taxis to the Lewis home and often helped with radio communication in the early days.

The understanding and cooperative U.S. embassy[11] team in Nairobi was a crucial source of support for Teresa. They willingly bent the rules to allow her in the restricted communications area for our daily radio chats. They received and read faxes to me over the radio and often lent a word of encouragement. After the genocide was over, I visited the embassy, and they gave me a very moving welcome, inviting everyone to come out of their offices and greet "76" ("76" was my radio handle that they all knew me by during the genocide).

### A Pillar of Strength

Teresa managed to make life more of an adventure than an ordeal for our children. She always found time to take them for a swim at a nearby hotel or shopping at Ya Ya's (a local mall). She

---

[11] Four years later the embassy in Nairobi was bombed, leaving over 200 people dead and 4,000 wounded. It would be the first time that many Americans would hear the name Osama bin Laden.

admits to the fact that the kids got a few more candy bars than normal.

It still amazes me when I think of her setting up house in a strange city, doing laundry in the guest room bathtub till her hands were raw, homeschooling Mindy and Lisa, sending money and supplies to me, corresponding with family and friends in the U.S., never missing a day on the radio! Some days we talked for hours over the radio waves, and never once did she give the impression that she had other things to do. I was often pinned down in the house by gunfire and mortars, not able to leave, and was so grateful to hear her sweet voice calling over the radio—

"76, 76, this is Tango Whiskey, do you copy?" [12]

No doubt she had a thousand other things pressing on her, but she gave no hint of needing to hurry. Selflessly, she gave me unwavering, rock-solid support while helping our children feel safe. So much credit goes to her during that time of being both mom and dad to our children and helping them understand why I stayed. They never showed any signs of insecurity or feeling abandoned by me.

Thirteen years earlier I had asked Teresa if she would marry me. We had met in high school, and I proposed on the verge of our graduation from college. Without hesitation she had said, "Yes, I will go anywhere in the world with you!" Neither one of us could have imagined where that *yes* would lead us. When you ask Teresa about her ability to maintain her sanity during those incredibly challenging months of 1994, she will gladly tell you about her faith in God.

\* \* \*

## Choices

Holocaust survivor and author Viktor Frankl writes about choice and dignity in his book *Man's Search for Meaning*:

---

[12] "76" had been my radio name for our home base for years, and "Tango Whiskey" was simply Teresa Wilkens' initials in radio talk.

… I may give the impression that the human being is completely and unavoidably influenced by his surroundings. (In this case the surroundings being the unique structure of camp life, which forced the prisoner to conform his conduct to a certain set pattern.) But what about human liberty? Is there no spiritual freedom in regard to behavior and reaction to any given surroundings? Is that theory true which would have us believe that man is no more than a product of many conditional and environmental factors—be they of a biological, psychological, or sociological nature? Is man but an accidental product of these? Most important, do the prisoners' reactions to the singular world of the concentration camp prove that man cannot escape the influences of his surroundings? Does man have no choice of action in the face of such circumstances?

We can answer these questions from experience as well as on principle. The experiences of camp life show that man does have a choice of action. There were enough examples, often of a heroic nature, which proved that apathy could be overcome, irritability suppressed. Man can preserve a vestige of spiritual freedom, of independence of mind, even in such terrible conditions of psychic and physical stress.

We who lived in concentration camps can remember the men who walked through the huts comforting others, giving away their last piece of bread. They may have been few in number, but they offer sufficient proof that everything can be taken from a man but one thing: the last of the human freedoms—to choose one's attitude in any given set of circumstances, to choose one's own way.

And there were always choices to make. Every day, every hour, offered the opportunity to make a decision, a decision which determined whether you would or would not submit to those powers which threatened to rob you of your very self, your inner freedom; which determined whether or not you would become the plaything of circumstance, renouncing freedom and dignity to become molded into the form of the typical inmate.

Seen from this point of view, the mental reactions of the inmates of a concentration camp must seem more to us than the mere expression of certain physical and sociological conditions. Even though conditions such as lack of sleep, insufficient food, and various mental stresses may suggest that the inmates were bound to react in certain ways, in the final analysis it becomes clear that the sort of person the prisoner became was the result of an inner decision, and not the result of camp influences alone. Fundamentally, therefore, any man can, even under such circumstances, decide what shall become of him—mentally and spiritually. He may retain his human dignity even in a concentration camp. (2006 ed., p. 65, 66)

Chapter 6

# BBC World Service

The BBC World Radio Service was of immeasurable value to me in staying connected to the outside world. On several occasions while listening to the BBC, I pushed the "record" button on my radio cassette player. These broadcasts also gave me a picture of what was happening in Rwanda that was much larger than the view I had looking out my living room window. I've included a transcription of a broadcast made on April 24:

**BBC Announcer**: *Lindsey Hilsum, who is now in Burundi, went up to the border to see the people fleeing the massacres. I asked her how many she thinks have come across.*

**Lyndsey Hilsum**: *Aid workers think that about 50,000 refugees have come across. But many more have been killed on the way; tens of thousands have been killed on the way. Those who are managing to get to Burundi are in a terrible state. Yesterday morning I went up to the border early in the morning and saw the first few who had crossed. There was a man and a woman; they were just sitting in the hut on the border. The man was crouching on the floor just shivering with terror. He had what looked like a grenade wound above one eye; he was just dripping blood and gibbering. And the woman, when she moved her headscarf, had a terrible bullet wound in her head. I was with some aid workers, and we took them to a hospital in the nearby town of Kayanza. There they treated more than 400 Rwandan refugees, many of whom had bullet wounds, grenade wounds, machete wounds. All these are Tutsis, and the Hutu militia who are killing and injuring these people say that one way you can tell a Tutsi is because Tutsis have longer fingers. So they are slicing off the fingers of children.*

**Announcer**: *Now who's organizing the killing? Because even if it started out as a spontaneous ethnic upsurge, one group against another, that cannot be sustained. If it's still going on like this it must be organized. Who is doing it?*

**Lyndsey Hilsum**: *I think it was organized from the beginning from the evidence which I've been gathering over the past few weeks. Certainly the refugees I've spoken to and the last few foreigners to leave Rwan-*

da say that the Burgermeister, who is the government-appointed local official, has been instrumental in organizing the massacre. I spoke to somebody who speaks very good Kinyarwanda, who intercepted radio conversation between people in the army and district officials giving instructions on where massacres should be carried out and who should be targeted.

**Announcer**: Is this some final solution to the ethnic squabble that's been in the country for hundreds of years? Are the Hutus trying to kill all the Tutsis?

**Lyndsey Hilsum**: Certainly that's what the Tutsis in Burundi think. I spoke to several refugees who said there aren't going to be any Tutsis left in Rwanda. There are a few like them who have escaped, and the rest have been killed. And certainly that appears to be the aim. The militia are organized by these officials in the military, the Interahamwe, and they are Hutu extremist militia; certainly their aim appears to be to exterminate Tutsis. It seems that genocide is definitely being committed in Rwanda at the moment.[13]

---

[13] Note that the term *genocide* is being used here 17 days after the president's plane was shot down. Thousands upon thousands of people have already been killed.

Chapter 7

# Soldiers Next Door

It must have been about the second week of the genocide that I got the idea of talking on cassettes to record what was happening around me. I honestly did not know if I was going to survive this dark time, and if I didn't survive I wanted to leave something for my wife and our three children. Perhaps hearing me tell stories would remind Teresa why we both decided that I should stay in Rwanda. Maybe the stories would help our children understand something more of their dad. Above all I wanted these stories to help the four of them know that I really did love them more than anything else.

I always scribbled our home address in Spokane, Washington, on each tape in the hope that if something did happen to me and our home here was looted, some kind person might find the tapes and send them to their intended destination. The vast majority of this book is based on these tapes, about eight hours of recordings.

The following is a transcription of an early tape from the first three weeks when I was confined to the house by the genocidal government's 24/7 curfew. The only people on the streets were the ones perpetrating the killing.

**Tape, April 19**
*Dear Teresa,*

*Today's been relatively quiet in terms of gunfire, and I've been doing more reading. Lying in the hallway was getting old, so I dragged a mattress into our bedroom to the spot between the bed and the closet: a bit sheltered, and different scenery. I hadn't been there long when I heard a shot and a thud that sounded like bricks crumbling. I waited fifteen minutes and everything remained quiet, so I silently crept outside for a look around. Sure enough, a stray bullet had slammed into our bedroom wall. I'm not saying this to cause any worry, seeing as how no one will listen to this tape until it's all over and I'm safe back together with you, Mindy, Lisa, and Shaun.*

*Oh, but I've got to tell you about yesterday, the 18th. Around one or two o'clock, I went outside and found Janvier sitting out front of the house in full view of the street. You know how many gaps there are* in the chainlink fence, where the reeds have been pulled out, and our gate of metal bars is now missing reeds for privacy as well. Basically, anyone walking by could look up the driveway and see this slender Tutsi boy sitting in plain sight.

I have not made a big deal about him hiding from our neighbors; they all pretty much know who is in the house. But to sit in plain view of the gate, for any stranger walking by to see, was too much. He was putting all our lives in danger. Angry people, violent people, people with assault rifles and people with homemade, deadly weapons were walking up and down the streets.

Before I pointed all of this out to Janvier, though, I did ask him how he was doing. Not knowing if his family was dead or alive obviously gave him plenty of reason to be depressed. He didn't respond to my question, and I thought to myself, despondent or not, the boy must behave responsibly, not only for his sake but for all our sakes. I suggested that he move his chair to a corner of the veranda where he would not be visible from the gate, and he quietly complied.

While pausing on the veranda, explosions on a far mountainside caught our attention. Looking across the valley and past the city, I could see big puffs of smoke rising high above Kigali, followed five or ten seconds later by earthshaking booms. They were bombing the restaurant/hotel L'Horizon.[14]

Later that afternoon we had visitors just a few feet away on the left side of our front yard fence. Normally, there were several families living in a collection of about five adobe brick tin-roofed homes there. These days, just one mom and a couple of kids remained. Six or seven soldiers decided to move into one of the empty houses right up against our fence. They brought a couple of cases of beer and perhaps a goat or two to have a barbecue.

I found out they were there when Janvier came walking in the back door with a sheepish look on his face. Looking both confused and frightened, he said some soldiers had seen him through the fence and started shouting about Tutsi sympathizers. After Pastor Seraya questioned Janvier, in order to be crystal clear about what had happened and who had said what, we decided that Mrs. Seraya would casually go to the fence and talk to the soldiers.

She has already proved to be an incredible peacemaker. She is so gifted when talking with impossibly difficult people. Anyone could see what a deadly threat these soldiers posed to us. Imagine trying to just

---

[14] This hotel belonged to our recently assassinated president's family, and my own family used to go up there to celebrate birthdays and other special occasions around the sparkling swimming pool. The panoramic view from up there was fantastic.

keep your voice steady in order to calm them. Perhaps she saw them more as sons and nephews than as torturing killers. I shake my head as I think about the courage it took to look square into their beery, blood-shot eyes.

Nonchalantly walking through the yard, she approached the fence and engaged one of the soldiers in conversation. "What's this nonsense about Tutsi sympathizers?" she asked. "Don't be ridiculous, we are not involved." It soon became clear that the soldiers wanted to see every-one in our house for themselves. She said, "Fine, come on around to the gate. I will let you in." As she met the soldiers down at the gate, Anitha came silently through the house to the back patio where Janvier was. You could see it in their eyes; they both believed that their worst fears were about to happen.

Pastor Seraya walked on down the driveway to the gate to join in the conversation. Looking out of the living room window, I weighed whether my presence would make things better or complicate the is-sue. Pastor and Mrs. Seraya were definitely the two best people to handle this situation, but it was tough waiting, doing nothing. The next moment Pastor Seraya was coming in from the front porch, asking for the gate key. I went to Janvier in the back yard to get the key, and then I walked back down the driveway with the pastor. I held the key visible in one hand, as I took hold of the gate with the other, but I didn't yet unlock the padlock.

"How are you doing?" they asked me.

"Not so good," I replied. "These are really difficult times."

"Yeah, really difficult times," they echoed. "Who do you have in your house, how many people?"

"Well . . ." I started to count in French holding up one, two, three fingers, and then I switched to English to make sure I was right as I reached "Seven."

Mrs. Seraya also said "Seven" in Kinyarwanda.

"Do you have any sympathizers or anything like that?"

"No, monsieur, I just have this family here, and I'm the director of ADRA. I've been in Rwanda for four years. This is my country, and I didn't evacuate with the other people because I came here to live with the people no matter what. You know ADRA is a humanitarian organi-zation, and we have been building schools and operating clinics. Pas-tor Seraya here is the legal representative of the Seventh-day Adventist Church and he is staying with me along with some workers."

They relaxed a bit, and we talked for another ten minutes or so. They didn't mention coming in anymore; in fact, they were polite and decent. There were four of them, with their machine guns over their shoulders, and we continued talking through the gate. Eventually we

*wished them courage in their work and told them that we were all pray-*
*ing for peace. Reaching through the bars, we shook each soldier's hand*
*and said our goodbyes. When they finally turned and walked away, a*
*collective sigh poured out as the three of us silently turned back towards*
*the house and headed up the driveway on shaky legs. We walked in the*
*front door and out the back to let Anitha and Janvier know that the sol-*
*diers were not coming in. Stepping back inside, we instinctively formed*
*a prayer circle.*

*This seemed to be a changing point for Janvier. As I said earlier, he*
*had every right to feel hopeless, not knowing the fate of his mom, dad,*
*little brothers, and sisters. It must have been especially tormenting won-*
*dering if he should try and do something, anything, no matter how des-*
*perate, to be there for his family, to somehow try and protect them. But*
*today he definitely saw how his actions affect the people around him.*

*Some days earlier he had asked a neighbor lady to try and con-*
*vince her husband, a gendarme (French for* policeman*), to take him to*
*his family's home to find out what had happened to them. Right after*
*the plan was made, however, the lady fled, and Janvier had no way of*
*contacting the gendarme again.*

*Bombs have been whistling overhead a good part of today. The*
*BBC said that a rocket had fallen in Amahoro Stadium, where the UN*
*is looking after thousands of people. According to the BBC, the rocket*
*killed 20 people and injured 14 others. I also saw people walking in the*
*valley today with sacks of beans on their heads. Evidently they had*
*been able to get into another warehouse. These warehouses are in a*
*no-man's land between the battle lines of the RPF and the Rwandan*
*government soldiers. Often the fighting is so intense that thieves can't*
*get access to warehouses. Every once in a while, though, there is a lull*
*in the fighting, and people get into yet another un-looted warehouse. In*
*a sense, the violence meters access to the food stocks.*[15]

*Towards evening there was a rap on the gate, which could have*
*meant just about anything. This time, though, it was only a man want-*
*ing to know what the medicine he held in his hand was for. All kinds of*
*"unidentified" things were being looted from the homes of foreigners.*
*This guy was hoping that the medicine he had stolen would be useful*
*for cuts, but it was only sore throat syrup.*

[15] When the genocide began there were more than 900,000 displaced
people in Rwanda as a result of the civil war that had gone on for three
years. There were also 350,000 refugees in Rwanda who had fled the
violence in Burundi to the south. Humanitarian organizations had warehouses with food stocks for these 1.25 million displaced/refugee persons.
Those food stocks are what fed the city of Kigali throughout its three-
month slaughter.

Chapter 8

# Trapped at Home

**Tape, April 19**

*Dear Teresa,*

*Talk about cabin fever. We've been unable to leave the house for days, and I am filled with the feeling that I should be doing more, that I should be out there. I'm trying to keep myself ready, so when the opportunity to go out and help people comes, I can move. I want to be ready to move.*

*Being trapped here at the house is a lot more frustrating than I would have ever imagined. When I look around, though, and see the other people in our home, I know I have a mission right here. A mission not only about being here for them, but also recognizing that what I'm going through now will somehow help me to better understand the people here and how their experiences shape the decisions they make, even during peacetime. No doubt this period stuck indoors is shaping and changing me as well.*

*I'm pretty sure I've read every book in the house. I've read everything from heroes of the French resistance during WWII to stories of American police officers killed in the line of duty.* Bible Smuggler *by Brother Andrew sure did trigger some interesting thoughts. The section in which he takes one of his Bibles out and puts it on the front seat next to him before driving up to the border post—to remind himself who was* really getting him through the borders with his so-called contraband—really blew me away. He gave all credit to God.

Though I have read Corrie Ten Boom's The Hiding Place *several times* during my life, it has taken on a different meaning and affected me on deeper levels because of what's happening to the Tutsi people. I am so moved by Corrie and her family's faith and courage; moved by their ingenuity in hiding Jewish people; moved by the strong, selfless spirit shown during the time she spent in the Holocaust camps. She and those she writes about were simply astounding,

You might be wondering how the animals are surviving all of this. Saturday afternoon, near the end of a Bible study, we heard a terrible racket coming from the garage. I had put the dogs in there because the rockets and gunfire scared them. As soon as I opened the door to see what the racket was about, Bimbi came side-winding out of there like a rocket. She moved like her back end was out of alignment, and you could see a wet patch on her rear that turned out to be gasoline from some bottles she must have knocked over. It was burning her skin! Fortunately there happened to be water in the pipes right then, so I was able to hose her off. Blackie was running circles around us, worried about Bimbi.

Poacher's rope broke the other day, though he didn't know it. He was still hanging on the burglar bars of the girls' bedroom window. Anitha and Mrs. Seraya came to get me, afraid that he would run away if they approached him, and while the monkey fascinates them, I think they are still not sure just how tame he is. And then there's the cat, who saunters around while bombs explode and guns fire in the background, acting as if it's all just a normal day. The two chickens don't seem to be flustered by the battle either.

## When Will This End?

Teresa,

Some of the explosions we have been hearing are the sound of rockets hitting the military camp in the center of town. They are usually shot three or four in succession, a long whistling sound followed by a few seconds of silence and then boom, boom, boom, boom! We can usually see a plume of smoke before we hear the boom. I don't know for sure, but I think the RPF is launching them from where they are stationed, about four or five blocks behind our home.

Not too long ago I talked by radio with Wayne Ulrich. He is always so encouraging. He's hoping to get MSF back in Kigali as soon as possible.

I'm so incredibly grateful we have the radio, Teresa; I can't imagine what this experience would be like without it! Even with the radio, though, there are certain things that are very hard to communicate. It seems like no one on the outside gets why we decided that I should stay. Why aren't the reasons we came to Rwanda in the first place and the responsibilities we feel towards Anitha and Janvier sufficient explanations by themselves? But you, Teresa, my Teresa, have been so good and strong through all of this, and I miss you so badly, and I miss the kids. I'm just sitting here holding a pillow, wishing it was all of you!

Not knowing how long this all will last is hard, really hard. It's been thirteen days since it all started, and nine days since I've seen any of you. Let's see, you left on Sunday morning of last week, and today is day ten away from the family. Not knowing how long and when we'll be together again is tough, flat out tough. There is no indication of which way the fighting is going. Part of the time the gunfire is between the RPF and the government soldiers (I don't know who is winning there), and part of the time it's the shooting of the Tutsi people.

The BBC didn't say anything yesterday about Rwanda, and today they just mentioned that a rocket landed in the stadium where the UN is sheltering people. Radio Rwanda reported that a new prefect for Kigali was appointed yesterday, Colonel Tharcisse Renzaho. It also said religious leaders had gathered in Gitarama, trying to figure out how to respond to the situation. Looting is still going on; I saw a wheelbarrow going down the road yesterday with a stove in it. It's just complete chaos.

Last Sunday's gun battle was probably our longest one so far, about four hours, from two o'clock till sundown. Heavy, heavy fighting all around the house, some big explosions that made the ceiling shake. I just lay on the mattress in the hallway with my Bible on my chest, repeating different Psalms and trying to think of songs, like "A Mighty Fortress is our God" and other good old favorites while things roared around us.

As the gunfire was heating up I couldn't help but peek out the window every so often, and I saw mothers and children running down the street. I could tell the action was moving in our direction, but from where? People were running this way and that; everyone seemed very confused.

The shooting lightened a bit, and I crept to the window for another look. This time I saw a soldier walking down the road. His black beret made me think he might be RPF, but a little later I peeked out again and saw a couple of men that were definitely Rwandan government soldiers going the other direction. They strolled along with their machine guns slung casually over their shoulders, as if the whole war was miles and miles away. Such strange warfare. I've been spared from seeing any *casualties up close, but the sounds have been terrible. Yesterday was relatively quiet, today much more frantic. It's strange, but lately the quieter things get, the uneasier I become, wondering what's coming next.*

*Yesterday morning I had clear radio reception with the ADRA/ South Sudan office and a great visit with Mitch Scoggins. What a good guy, and someone you can really count on.*

*I hadn't talked to the embassy people in Nairobi for several days and was feeling good about being able to get through to them yesterday. There's a guy stationed there who does radio communications and has the initials EV for Echo Victor; he's such a kind and encouraging man. I hope I can meet him when this thing is over. He has never voiced an opinion about my decision to stay; he just gives consistent support.*

*I mention this because the Burundi U.S. embassy radioman did have an opinion, which he shared when I talked to him yesterday. While he was putting through a radio/telephone patch to you, I asked him what the Burundi embassy's position was right then on evacuation of staff. He said they were on ordered departure. Their staff was greatly reduced as well as was the USAID staff. Then he added, "You would make things a whole lot easier on your family if you came out." I thanked him for the update and for helping me get through to you. The conversation got me thinking about how quickly I sometimes form opinions as soon as I learn about something. I've decided I would do well to be slower in forming opinions and faster in looking for the different sides and components of any situation.*

## Nine Lives: Chance or Something Else
*Teresa,*

*As I lay in the hallway last night, trying to fall asleep after blowing out my candle, I thought about our morning radio conversation. Remember we spoke of how, from a normal perspective, the longer this fighting drags out, the more likely it is that there might be some kind of tragedy?* (We didn't talk directly about dying.) *Kind of like Russian roulette: sooner or later one spin is going to leave a bullet in the chamber.*

*And yet we were discovering a different perspective. I recall how we decided that, if our security is really coming from faith in God, it doesn't matter if we're at risk for twenty seconds or twenty minutes or twenty months. His protection will not change. But then what about those . . . got to switch off.*

*Sleep, sleep, got to sleep.*
*Good night. Love you!*

My understanding of God's protection is constantly expanding. Lately I've been thinking that God's plan of protection doesn't revolve exclusively around miraculous interventions on his part. Perhaps his plan of protection includes a component, a potentially huge component, that involves life choices, a philosophy of choices that might be called "other-focused" choices. A life philosophy that says, "I will experience authentic security when I choose to care for others first instead of expecting to be cared for." Or in a slightly different vein, "Security comes when I choose to live a cooperative style of life instead of a competitive style." But terrible stuff still happens—someone who has chosen to live this "other-focused" way is killed, and I ask myself and others how it could have been different? Has that person been betrayed? By whom? Are we somehow guilty?

## Patrick Battening Down the Hatches at the Red Cross

### Tape, April 21

*Morning, Teresa,*

*I don't know if you can hear that rumbling in the background, but it's been quite a morning! I woke up with mortars exploding all around. None were really close to the house; well, maybe one or two were close, and they were followed by periodic rifle fire quite close to the house. Honestly, though, most of the heavy fighting is on the other side of the valley towards town. The BBC just announced on the radio that General Dallaire said the town of Byumba is now in the hands of the RPF.*

*Yesterday morning I had a radio visit with Patrick, the logistics man at the International Committee of the Red Cross (ICRC). From our house I can see their compound on the other side of the valley. He told me to contact him whenever I needed. He also advised me to keep my head down. Armed militias are still moving around town, and he said they are extremely aggressive. In short, he left little doubt that we should still remain inside.*

*I talked to him again this morning, and he said that yesterday one of their warehouses was looted. I think that four or five of theirs are still safe. Today he was going to work on getting more security for his warehouses and his vehicles. It sounded like he was battening down the hatches to settle in for the long haul, assessing what they still had available and trying not to lose any more.*

Patrick confirmed what I had heard about the ADRA warehouses being on fire two days ago, though he couldn't give details on it, so I don't know the extent of the damages. I hope it's not too bad.

It appears that most of Kigali, including all of us here, are surviving on goods looted from warehouses like ADRA's, the Red Cross's, and other aid organizations. Mrs. Seraya buys stolen lentils over the fence in the back yard, along with toilet paper and propane bottles for cooking. It feels like the market is coming to us. Glad I like lentils, though I never thought I would be eating them every day.

Chapter 9

# A Matter of Conscience

The following is the transcript of a letter that Teresa read to me over the radio on April 21 from the Seventh-day Adventist Church world president, expressing his desire for me to evacuate immediately.

*Dear Carl,*

*I have tried various means to communicate with you personally and orally, but it has not been possible under the present conditions.*

*Thus I must resort to the written word. Your total commitment and dedication is both heroic and exemplary. Needless to say, I, and my fellow leaders appreciate you, and what you have accomplished. However, it is for this very reason that I am asking you to depart Kigali as soon as possible.*

*It goes against my very nature to use the word* order *in this context; however, that is the word that most accurately describes the sense that I must convey. I am aware that most of the UN personnel have left the area, and therefore expect you to determine a reasonably safe method of evacuation.*

*We must use your skills and knowledge to define future work in Rwanda. Therefore we are asking that you immediately relocate to Nairobi to work with others there in the vital look-ahead plans.*

*Your remaining in Kigali would deny the church and ADRA the input which you could provide, and can be counterproductive. For the greater good of the cause, I want you to lay down the good work you have been doing in Kigali in order to become part of the larger task ahead.*

*This directive* [static in the radio transmission, but I think *directive* is the word used] *is given after much prayer and consultation. It is a decision, not a request. Please contact us immediately upon reaching Nairobi. Our prayer is that Christ will be with you and protect you as you relocate.*

*Yours in Christ,*
*Robert S. Folkenberg*
*President of the General Conference of Seventh-day Adventists*

I don't have further recordings or recollections of further conversation between Teresa and me about this letter. Later that day

I typed the letter out from the recording I'd made, so I could have it in hard copy to study and prepare a response. Although I don't have a copy of my response or a radio recording of my dictating it to Teresa, I remember writing something close to the following:

*Dear Elder Folkenberg,*

*Thank you very much for your letter. I am not refusing to obey your directive, but I need your help with two things before I can comply.*

*First, I need your help telling my friends and Rwandan coworkers that God will be with them and protect them, and explain to them why I can't stay and rely on that same presence and protection.*

*Secondly, I need your help in making arrangements for the safeguarding of the two young people in my home who have Tutsi ID cards that will surely lead to them being killed.*

*As soon as you are able to help me with these two things I will be glad to join my family in Nairobi.*

*Sincerely,*
*Carl Wilkens*

## April 22

I remember lying in the hallway listening to the BBC and hearing that Richard Nixon died. Later that day a communication officer at the U.S. embassy in Nairobi read to me the second and final letter from Elder Folkenberg's office. Here is a transcription of the recording of that conversation:

**Embassy officer:** *. . . and it's written by Gerry Karst, special assistant to the president, dated April 22, 1994. How copy?*

**Carl:** *Good copy, go ahead, over.*

**Embassy officer:**

*Dear Carl,*

*Elder Folkenberg is on a trip to the South Pacific and not available for comment. However, a group of church leaders have studied your response and on behalf of the world Church have prepared the following response.*

*Elder Folkenberg has clearly indicated his decision that you leave*

*Kigali. We wish you were safe with your family. However, since you have a compelling reason for remaining, we have no intention of forcing you to violate your conscience. Therefore, we have nothing further to urge.*

*Please know that we are deeply concerned for your safety, and we urge you to exercise extreme caution in attempting to move about. Your church family is upholding you constantly in prayer, asking our heavenly Father to bring a positive end to the crisis.*

*Sincerely,*
*Gerry Karst*
*Special Assistant to the President*

**Embassy officer:** *How copy? Over.*

**Carl:** *Good Copy. Thanks so much!*

*Well,* I thought with a smile, *that sounds different from the first letter. It's good that they "have no intention of forcing me to violate my conscience."*

After listening to the recording of this transmission several times, I decided they were not looking at the decision Teresa and I made as insubordination but as a matter of conscience. Following our conscience is what it really boils down to. I believe in the end we answer to one Person, and that is God. All of my security, all of my strength, all of my ability to do anything comes from God. In the years since the genocide I've come to the conclusion that God supplies these three things—security, strength, and ability—less through miraculous interventions and more through ordinary people, the laws of nature, and the simple laws of God. Laws such as, "Treat others as you would like to be treated" and "Love your enemies." Simple laws like those.

### No Risk Meter

More taped journal transcripts:

*This morning was another fabulous conversation with Teresa! Have I said before how much I love talking to Teresa on the radio? She is just incredible. Like no other woman. I am just so thankful that God has given her the same peace that he has given me during this horrific time, and that we have the radio to make the distance shorter. There has got to be a reason for everything we go through, and it will contribute to some work in the future. I just pray that the rest of our family can have the same peace that God has given Teresa and me. I hate for anyone to spend time in the darkness of doubt.*

*God's protection came up in this morning's conversation with Teresa. Lately I've been thinking that God does not rate risk on a scale of 1 to 10. For example, walking across the street would be a level "1" and being in a place with mortars falling all around would be a level "10." This is our way of looking at risk and security, but with God I don't think there is any scale. If God wants me to be on a plane, crossing the street, kayaking in Hell's Canyon, or on a battlefield, the security component of those experiences doesn't really enter into the decision from His perspective. It seems silly to think that God would find some situations more difficult than others to provide protection in. Things become more complicated when my wants and power of choice enter into the equation. However, picturing God operating without a "risk meter" in hand is something to think about.*

*The key players in this struggle are supposed to be meeting in Arusha today to work out some plan to end this madness. I hope it's happening, not that anyone is expecting miracles, but perhaps something will change that will bring peace back to this country, to this land. And, yes, maybe some of us are expecting miracles.*

### Five Spanish Sisters of Charity

*Today I had the interesting role of playing radio middleman between a Mother Superior in Nairobi and the Red Cross here in Kigali. Mitch had passed the message on to me, and I asked the Red Cross to pass it on to UNAMIR. Mother Superior wants to get five Spanish Sisters of Charity out of Rwanda.[16] The compound they live and work on is near Holy Family Church (a Catholic church where hundreds of people had taken refuge), just a few blocks from the Mille Collines Hotel. There were said to be 20 Rwandan sisters working with these expatriates.*

*Unwilling to abandon the orphans and elderly folks they were caring for, these sisters had refused to be evacuated with the other for-*

---

[16] There were what I call ten easily identifiable foreigners that I know of who did not evacuate from Kigali: Five Catholic sisters from Spain, two Catholic fathers from Germany and France, a Frenchman named Marc Vaiter who had orphans in his home, a Swissman named Philippe Gaillard who headed the Red Cross, and myself.

eigners two weeks earlier. I asked Mitch to pass back to the Mother Superior different stories of courageous actions taken by Rwandans, like our neighbors, to save lives. It's important for the world to know that even though there are so many terrible stories coming out of Rwanda, it is still possible for a person to make a difference for good here.

Mother Superior had gotten word that UNAMIR was aware of the location of her nuns, and they had even been to their compound to evacuate them earlier. But the sisters had refused to come out and unlock the gates. This time the order from Mother Superior to evacuate came with the instructions that UNAMIR should break down the gates if necessary. I have to confess that I only passed on the order to evacuate and left out the part about bashing in the gates. It looks like I'm not the only one getting pressure to leave.

Those Spanish sisters stayed throughout the whole genocide, and their actions were a real inspiration to me. One day I witnessed an incident showing their courage and determination. They had a small stub-nosed truck, where the engine is located under the cab, and the windshield was either shot or busted out. I can still picture two petite sisters dressed in their habits, driving up to a roadblock manned by the Interahamwe. They were on their way to collect water for the orphans, and these thugs began to hassle them. I was on the other side of the roadblock and watched a couple of guys walk up to the front of the sisters' little truck and poke their automatic weapons right through the opening where the windshield should have been. They held their gun barrels inches from the sisters' noses. The sisters sat perfectly still, not batting an eye. They were willing to wait the men out. Eventually the Interahamwe backed down and let them through.

People ask, "Where was God during the genocide?" I say, look at these sisters—their supernatural strength and love, the way they followed their conscience—and it answers the God question for me; well, not completely, but it begins to answer the God question.

# Chapter 10
# **Heri**

Several years after moving to Rwanda, I came home from work one day to find that our kids had made an exciting discovery. "Dad, did you know that there's an orphanage three houses down?" they asked. "Thirty kids and a lot of them are babies! We were playing with them all afternoon."

During the early days of the genocide, when all the foreigners had fled Rwanda, the couple in charge of the orphanage down the street left as well. I shake my head and am staggered by the thought of what would be involved in making a decision to leave thirty children, little ones from the age of five years down to four months.

These kids had already been dealt harsh blows and were now being orphaned again. Our neighbors thought that the couple running the orphanage were Belgian. Did the team at the Belgian embassy, who was in charge of evacuating all their citizens, have any moral obligation to these children after evacuating their guardians?

In any case, let me tell you what I know about the man who refused to leave Rwanda and these children. His name is Heri.

On April 26, I asked Mrs. Seraya if she had any news about the orphanage three doors down from us. "Yes," she said. "It's still there and functioning."

*That's a relief,* I thought.

A little later Mrs. Seraya announced, "The man from the orphanage is here."

"OK," I said, "What's up?"

"I sent word that you wanted to talk to him," she replied.

"Oh, OK," I said, with a surprised smile. It's not that I didn't want to talk to him; it's just that I felt pretty empty, knowing I didn't have anything I could give him for the kids.

Walking down to the gate, I met Heri for the first time, and he began to tell me the orphans' story. He was the manager of the orphanage now, but before the evacuation of the couple in charge, he had been the night watchman.

"You and I are the only ones left on this street," he said, referring to our being the only people on our street still living in the western-style homes. He told me about the first three days when he had been left all alone with the thirty little ones. Already I could tell I was going to really like this guy.

Heri now had four or five women helping him, so the hands-on care of the children was more manageable. What really had him concerned was the impossible task of protecting the orphans from the fighting going on in our neighborhood.

At this point in our conversation he motioned toward the policeman in uniform standing quietly next to him and said, "This is my friend." The gendarme asked me several questions about who I was and who was living in our home. I told him about the Serayas and me.

"How is security?" I asked. "Is it possible to move around town yet?"

"It's getting better," he responded. "You just have to have a laissez passé[17] to be out on the streets."

"Oh," I said slowly. "How and where do I get that?"

"You go to the prefecture building," he said.

"So I can just drive to the prefecture building?" I asked, raising my eyebrows.

"Well, I can take you tomorrow," he said with a smile.

I hadn't thought to ask him to do that, but since he offered, I agreed. "Yes, please, let's go."

This particular member of the gendarme was actually from the home commune of Mrs. Seraya, and she seemed to know a bit about him, which helped me lean toward trusting him. We all said goodbye, with plans to meet the next morning for a trip to the prefecture office.

It's a regret of mine that, throughout the genocide, I didn't take the opportunity to sit down and get to know Heri better. I could

[17] A government-issued pass.

have benefited from hearing his stories and learning more about the way he interacted with people. Instead, most of my conversations with this quiet man were usually about security and finding supplies for the orphans. My respect for Heri soon measured in the tons. I found his courage and diplomacy in dealing with the Interahamwe astounding.

I was so surprised the day I learned that Heri was a foreigner, or I should say he could have posed as a foreigner; he had identity documents from both Zaire and Burundi. Though he could have gotten help to leave the country with the other foreigners if he had wanted, he had chosen to stay. What a choice! It truly was a miracle that all but one of Heri's orphans survived.[18]

When my family and I returned to Rwanda after living in America for seven months following the end of the genocide, I found out Heri was without a job. I don't know where the orphans were moved to, but evidently there was no work for Heri. He came to me with an idea for a recycling business; he wanted to melt down scrap aluminum to make cooking pots. I gave him $300 to get started, our paths went different ways, and 18 months later my family moved back to America.

Fourteen years passed before I caught up with Heri again. It was July 2009, and he now had a good job as a watchman for an international organization in Kigali. When I got his cell phone number and heard his voice on the other end, all kinds of memories came flooding back. He generously agreed to meet with me and the eight genocide/holocaust educators I had brought to Rwanda. I was definitely excited to see Heri again. Powerful feelings welled up inside when I saw Heri's huge smile and heard his thoughtful, articulate responses to the teachers' questions (that same smile and diplomacy that served those orphans so well during the killing). One teacher asked him why he stayed when he could have so easily left. He sat quietly while thinking, and before he could answer someone added, "Do you think it was something your parents taught you?"

---

[18] Weeks before the genocide ended, a mortar landed in the front yard of the orphanage, killing one child and seriously injuring another.

Heri looked up and began speaking: "My parents died when I was seven. One of them was a Protestant and one was a Muslim, and I was then raised by Catholic fathers in an orphanage; I could pray with anyone!" he said with a warm grin. Then he added, "Perhaps it was partially due to the Catholic fathers' example that I stayed."

Later in our meeting, with all the teachers gathered around and little video cameras rolling, Heri told a story that perfectly illustrated how resourceful, determined, compassionate, and diplomatic he was. He told us how one day early on in the genocide he had managed to get a hefty supply of cooking oil, beans, and sugar from the Red Cross for the orphans in his care. It was so much food that he couldn't carry it all in one trip back to the orphanage. Heri was able to find a place where he could safely store the goods, so he put what he could manage in a sack on his head and filled his arms with sugar and cooking oil.

He was just getting underway on his nearly three mile hike when he was intercepted by one of the killing squads and robbed of everything. Heri turned around, went straight back to his stockpile, and again loaded himself up with as much as he could carry. This time he picked a different route, hoping to avoid another encounter with the roving killing squads. He nearly made it this time, but a few blocks from home he was surrounded by a gang who again stripped him of everything. It was too late in the day to try for a third trip, so Heri was forced to return home empty-handed and face the hungry, expectant looks of his thirty little ones with nothing to show for his efforts.

Early the next morning Heri was on the road back to his stockpile with another strategy. He sold some of this valuable food, and with the money he hired a car to transport the rest of it home. You can imagine the huge sigh of relief he must have breathed when his hired driver finally pulled into the driveway of the orphanage after successfully making it through so many roadblocks. Imagine the excitement of those kids! That night a gang, most likely tipped off by someone watching the car full of food drive into the orphanage, forced its way inside the gates and stole all the food that Heri had worked so incredibly hard to bring for his kids.

A teacher looked at Heri in wonder and asked if he had ever felt like giving up. I had been translating into French for Heri and then back to English, but when I heard this question I thought, *I can answer this question. Heri is no quitter.* I translated anyway and was shocked when Heri quietly said, "Yes, I did give up one day." I quickly translated his answer and then asked him, "Heri, what do you mean?"

"Well," he went on in his soft-spoken way, "one day it just got to be too much. I walked down the driveway, closed the gate behind me, and left the orphanage without any intention of going back. I walked and walked, eventually getting to the garden plots in the valley, and that's when it hit me. With every step it became clearer and clearer: *it was much harder to leave than to stay,* so I turned around and went back."

# Chapter 11
# **Roadblocks**

**April 27**

As I sat down on the couch in the living room to put on my shoes and socks, something didn't quite feel right. *What was it?* A few seconds after I finished putting my shoes on, it finally hit me: This was the first time I'd put shoes on my feet in three weeks. In fact, I hadn't even left the house since the president's plane was shot down on April 6, and even that event seemed like such a long time ago. It was strange how our home and little fenced-in yard had become a nest of security for the five of us (the Serayas' nephew and his wife had departed for another part of the country), and now I was planning on venturing outside the safety of our front gate. What would I find? How would I be treated? Would Janvier, Anitha, and Mrs. Seraya be safe while I was gone? These questions and many others filled my head as I finished tying my shoes.

At nine o'clock, we were still waiting for our police escort to arrive at our gate. Yesterday, Heri had introduced me to a gendarme who volunteered to escort Pastor Seraya and me to the center of town to get a laissez passé. Ten o'clock came and passed, and still there was no gendarme. At 10:30 Dassan, one of our ADRA employees, showed up at the gate, and I was more than happy to have him join us. He was ex-military and levelheaded, and in the past he and I had gotten through some tough scrapes together. We asked him about the level of violence around the city, and, based on his recommendations, Pastor Seraya and I decided to move ahead one step at a time and see how things would unfold.

Backing out of our driveway onto the dirt road, we knew that the first roadblock was less than 100 yards from our driveway. This barrier was operated by the Tailor Man, a man I had waved to several times a day for the last couple of years while he busily worked on his front porch with a foot-powered sewing machine.

He had always seemed like a nice, gentle guy, and it was strange to see him by the barrier with a weapon in his hand. He let us through without much trouble, but our troubles began at the next roadblock another 150 yards down the road. There were two barriers at this intersection: one to get into the intersection and another as we turned left to get out. They couldn't have been more than 25 feet apart. The Interahamwe at the first one weren't going to let us go through because we didn't have the laissez passé, but after explaining that we were on our way to get one, they finally said, "OK, you can go through." This allowed us to drive out into the intersection, where we had to stop immediately and go through the whole thing all over again to turn left.

The second barrier was facing downhill, and with the morning rains drenching the city, the unpaved road was slick. I managed to drive up to the barrier without sliding into anything. From the minute our car stopped, we were told we wouldn't be getting through without a laissez passé. We talked and talked but made no progress, so finally we just sat there quietly and waited. If you're smart in Africa, you learn to sit patiently and wait; something will eventually happen.

And eventually something did happen. The Interahamwe told us that if we could get a soldier to go with us, they would let us pass. A soldier happened to be walking by right at that moment, and maybe seeing him is what gave them the idea. They called him over, and immediately it became apparent that he *really, really* didn't want to get involved in this. Pastor Seraya explained our situation, but the soldier still refused to help.

"I'm not going to town. You know every soldier has his assigned duty to do, and this is not mine," the soldier said. What he said made sense, so we asked him to please help us talk our way through this barrier. After a serious conversation, the Interahamwe opened the barrier, and we went sliding through in our little Corolla.

I quickly lost the fight against both the angle of the road's slope and the pull of gravity. In no time we found ourselves sliding sideways until our car came to a stop in the ditch. The front wheels spun and spun, but there was no way we would get out under our own power. This wasn't the first time I had been stuck on that hill. There had been plenty of times in years past that I had to hire guys to push me out, even when driving a vehicle with four-wheel drive.

In times past, pushers always seemed to materialize when needed, and today was no exception. Just like old times, a gang of guys came running happily down the hill shouting, "We'll help! We'll help!" I shook my head in amazement as I watched them come from the very barrier where they had just hassled us so much!

If I didn't act quickly and pick four of them, the whole gang would be demanding payment, so I picked the biggest guys, and they pushed us out without much effort. Back on the road, I told them that I didn't have any money right then, but they could come to my house when I got back home later. Of course, they all knew where I lived.

The rest of the barriers were uneventful; we explained the same thing at each roadblock, sometimes taking longer if need be, telling them where we were going and letting them know I was the director of ADRA. At one roadblock, Pastor Seraya started to explain to the man who we were, and the guy growled, "I don't care who you are; I just want to see your ID cards!"

For so many, their ID cards decided whether they walked through that roadblock or were murdered on the spot and added to a lifeless pile of bodies. By the time I started moving around the city, however, most of the dead had been removed. We finally got through the last barrier and pulled into the parking lot of the prefecture office.

I didn't know it at the time, but this was the beginning of building a network of relationships, beginning with the Interahamwe on the street and going all the way up to the top leaders of the genocidal government. It would be these relationships that would enable us to accomplish the work that lay ahead. Often these relationships began in the unlikeliest of circumstances.

Finding our way to the right office, we asked the secretary how to apply for a laissez passé.

"That will be no problem," she said. "Just find a seat and wait here."

Pastor Seraya, Dassan, and I sat down with all the other people in the waiting room. Whether you were at a roadblock or sitting in a government office, it was strange and deeply troubling to see that so much order and structure was preserved during the genocide. Before long a military officer came in, a colonel, I guessed. I watched him move around the room, greeting different people for a few minutes, and I thought to myself, *He seems like a decent kind of guy.* Dassan leaned over and whispered in my ear, "That's the prefect, Tharcisse Renzaho." A prefect was the equivalent of a governor, and Prefect Renzaho had recently been put in charge of the greater Kigali area.

At one point, I caught his eye, and he nodded toward me while he continued dealing with other people. When he got to us, he said, "How are you? What can I do for you?" I explained to him that I was the director of ADRA, and then I introduced him to Pastor Seraya and Dassan. We had come for a laissez passé, and I wanted to ask how he felt ADRA as a humanitarian aid organization could best serve Kigali. Some days earlier on the radio he had announced that the Red Cross was the only aid organization that had not fled, and I wanted him to know that ADRA was still here.

"Very good, very good," he said. "Where have you been staying?"

"In my home in Kacyiru," I replied.

"That is very dangerous over there," he said. "You sleep there at night?"

"Actually, I haven't left my home in 21 days," I said.

"Oh my, well . . . anyway," he said, "now we will get you travel documents, no problem, and if you need any police or anything like that. . . ."

"In fact," I interrupted, "I would like to go down and visit the ADRA compound today."

"Okay," he replied. "I'll assign a police officer to go with you. We don't want these bandits to give you more trouble. I'm sorry to hear that ADRA was looted and at least one warehouse was burnt."

He then told one of his subordinates to get me a good policeman, "not just anyone, but a good one!" So we ended up with two commune policemen[19] as we headed toward ADRA. Little did we know that we would soon come under fire.

---

[19] A special branch of the police force that provides security for government buildings.

# Chapter 12
# **Building Our Network**

L eaving the prefecture office, we drove through the residential section of Kiyovu, one of the oldest sections of Kigali, where foreigners had lived for generations. It was eerie, a bit like a ghost town. Barriers and roadblocks were sparsely manned or completely vacant. I drove slowly and looked carefully around the empty barriers we encountered, making sure no one was going to shoot us. At one barrier, a man asked in English, "Are you American?" He had been a house worker for an American family in that neighborhood, and as we pulled away, I wondered what his memories were of the family he had worked for. I thought of Anitha and Janvier and their connections with our kids and wondered if this man had connections with foreign children. And if he did, were the foreign children thinking about him right now? Was anybody concerned for him right now?

Just above the Kiyovu Hotel and Le Petit Kigali, there was another man sitting on a couch alongside the road who looked familiar (there was a lot of upholstered furniture at the roadblocks). As the man sauntered over, I eyed his army fatigue jacket, blue jeans, and baseball cap. In his arms he cradled a little machine gun, which looked like a miniature weapon.

"Should be ADRA, is that not right?" he asked in French.

"Oui," I replied. "Hey, I know you, but from where? Oh yeah," I continued, "the car parts place."

He had been out of work, just like everybody else, and his new job was running a barrier. We had a friendly conversation before he told another guy to move the stick; barriers were sometimes made of car chassis, empty beer crates, tires, a tree trunk, or just a stick in the road.

On the way to ADRA, I made a quick stop at the ICRC. We parked outside because the two commune policemen with me had machine guns, which were not allowed on the Red Cross campus.

Climbing the steps to the entrance, I noticed several stacks of 100-pound sacks of food, serving as sand bags in front of the double glass doors. No doubt they would help stop bullets and shrapnel. Walking down the hallway, I could see that many of the offices had been converted into housing. A little boy, wearing only shorts, came walking out of one room.

Once inside, I got a hold of Patrick, the ICRC man I had been communicating with over the radio. His report was anything but encouraging. As the continuing violence restricted their activities more and more, the ICRC was forced to scale back their whole operation. One surgical team had been sent out of the country over the weekend after some volunteers of the Rwandan Red Cross staff had been killed. The neutrality of the Red Cross was not respected, and mortars from the RPF's assault on the Rwandan government were even landing on the well-marked ICRC compound. Over the weekend, there were several incidents of patients being pulled from Red Cross ambulances at roadblocks and killed in the middle of the road. Patrick said they had been forced to make the difficult decision to stop sending ambulances out to collect the wounded. Now the injured were on their own when it came to finding a way to reach the ICRC field hospital, which had been set up at the school next to their office headquarters.

I asked Patrick what they were able to do to stop the spread of disease from all the corpses.

"The only thing we can report," he said, "is that we give thirty liters of fuel a day to a city truck that goes around collecting bodies. Prisoners have been taken out of prison to do this work, along with digging mass graves."

People who were being treated at the Red Cross hospital couldn't be released because at the first roadblock outside the campus they would become patients again, or worse, which presented the ICRC with another problem: finding space for the newly admitted and newly released.

Before leaving, I had the opportunity to speak with the chief of the delegation, Philippe Gaillard.[20] Seeing the dark circles under his eyes, and the eyes of everyone else at the ICRC, for that matter, made me wonder if they ever slept. Their courage and dedication drove them relentlessly. A few people were making a difference. A few foreigners and a few Rwandans were making a difference together.

After leaving the Red Cross, we drove past the French school where, three weeks earlier, hundreds of foreigners had abandoned their vehicles. They boosted their families up into French and Belgian military transport trucks bound for the airport, where jets would take them to their homelands. The Interahamwe had managed to hot-wire most of the SUVs and sedans and used them to more speedily carry out their murderous work. A couple of people, lounging in the few remaining car shells, watched us drive by.

### One-Time Visit to the ADRA Compound

"Belge! Belge!" The gang shouted the French word for Belgian at me as we approached the last barrier before ADRA. I stopped next to an abandoned MSF vehicle on the shoulder, and they asked me, "You're not a Belgian, are you?"

"No, no, I'm an American," I replied.

"Well, lucky for you, that you're an American," one guy said, as he pulled a very long-bladed knife out of its sheath and waved it menacingly around. My eyes were fixed on the blade, gleaming in the sun, as he added, "Because if you were a Belgian, this is what would happen to you." He made a "ha, ha, ha" sound as he drew the knife across his own throat and walked away, ordering the barrier to be opened. It's mind-boggling to think of the festive attitude we often encountered at these barriers, and at the same time, to see how the people could be so cold-blooded one moment and in the next moment are helping to push your car out of a ditch.

The industrial park where the ADRA compound is located was a place I had always known as a buzzing hive of activity. But on

---

[20] You can read Philippe Gaillard's powerful testimony at: http://www.pbs.org/wgbh/pages/frontline/shows/ghosts/interviews/gaillard.html

this day, it appeared completely lifeless. Driving through ADRA's open gates, I zigged and zagged through our large parking area. It was covered with all kinds of garbage, papers, cooking oil cans, and debris spilling out of a recently arrived shipping container of medical supplies. After parking by the front office, I stepped out of the car and glanced back toward the entrance. There, sticking his head out of the guardhouse was Alfsa, our watchdog. He was terribly thin and skittish, but he came when I called. I locked him in his pen so that he wouldn't bother anyone while we looked around to see if there was anything salvageable.

Going from office to office, I could see that everything was either stolen or torn apart. I found six inches of soggy paper, computer discs, broken planters, and dirt on the floor, with puddles of water everywhere. The phone system, computer systems, desks, bookcases, and chairs had all been taken. The pharmacy we maintained to stock five clinics around the country was stripped bare. The looters had even taken the director's sign off my office door. The sinks busted off the bathroom walls were the source of all the water on the floor.

There wasn't a single piece of clothing left in the warehouse where we had previously stored hundreds of bales of clothes for people displaced by the three years of war. The food warehouses were empty except for a few busted-open and spoiled food sacks scattered here and there. All the welding, grinding, and metal shop equipment was also gone. The warehouse that had been used for years by the UNHCR (United Nations High Commissioner for Refugees) and the Red Cross had been set on fire and was completely destroyed. Metal beams buckled and sagged, and through the twisted metal roofing sheets, I could see the sky.

Simply put, there was nothing for us here. Gazing out over the lawn, I could picture the numerous staff picnics and three-legged races that had taken place there, and I wondered what it must have been like at the height of the looting. Where had Alfsa cowered while looters hit this place like a plague of locusts?[21]

Just then, shots were fired nearby, bringing me instantly back into the present. Was there anything else to check before leaving? I paused, and then remembered the fuel pumps by the gate. Halfway to the pumps, I was hit with an overpowering smell and almost vomited. Among the rubbish in the parking lot, I saw what Alfsa had been living off of: a man's bloated and partially eaten body. I called to the commune police, who had been poking around among the warehouses, to wait down by the gate. I would let the dog out, get the car, and come pick them up.

Dassan and I were walking toward the office when shots rang out again, this time much closer. Then a string of bullets came whistling through the compound and ricocheted off the shipping container next to us. Dassan dove for cover as I flattened myself against the wall. After a few seconds of silence, we dashed for the building.

When I let Alfsa out of his pen, he stuck to my heels like glue. I felt so guilty about leaving him, but he was a big dog, and there wasn't room for him and the commune police in my back seat. When I got home that evening, I put a partial bag of dog food in my car, hoping that one day I might be able to get back by ADRA. I was never able to, and I ended up with this little bit of dog food in my car throughout the genocide.

Looking at the ADRA sign in my rearview mirror as we left, I had a nauseous, empty feeling in the pit of my stomach. So many wonderful memories of school building projects, brainstorming sessions, logistical challenges overcome, late nights spent in the mechanics pit, funny cultural faux pas, clinic staffing dilemmas resolved, and many warm friendships developed there. All of them were now behind us as I swerved to the right and made way for the oncoming truck full of military soldiers racing toward us.

---

[21] A good friend pointed out how easy it is to use dehumanizing phrases like a "plague of locusts" when talking about the "other" —anyone we don't want to identify with. Is it worth the time to find other words to describe the looters and not compare them to a "plague of locusts"?

# Chapter 13
# **Happy Anniversary Mom and Dad**

When we got back to the center of town, Dassan and the commune policemen wanted to stop by the market. As we drove down the street, some of the shops looked trashed or totally destroyed, while others appeared to be untouched. Farther along, we saw the body of a man lying facedown in the street, with two portable stereos still clutched in his hands. It looked as if he had been murdered recently, and it felt so bizarre to find a market functioning at a time like this.

We paid our commune policemen a "thank you" fee while saying thanks and goodbye. I gave Dassan money to buy food for his family, and he headed to his home, which, thankfully, was not far from the market. Walking into the center of the market, I went looking for some tomatoes, carrots, and cucumbers. The cucumbers were too expensive, and I didn't find any tomatoes, but I did manage to buy a few carrots.

Pastor Seraya and I then drove the six or seven blocks to the church headquarters. The Swiss embassy shared one side of the city block with the church offices, and when we drove past it, we saw the smashed windows and broken furniture in the yard and knew that it, too, had been looted. With that fresh in our minds, we were expecting the worst as we stopped at the locked gates of the Rwanda Union Mission of Seventh-day Adventists.

The place was untouched, perfect, with not one broken window. In a back storeroom we collected a bag of charcoal and a couple of charcoal cookers that belonged to Pastor Seraya. While he retrieved some things from his office, I went exploring through the building. The electricity was out, so I didn't have much hope for the phone system, but I grabbed the receiver on the fax machine anyway and put it to my ear. There was a dial tone! Quickly dialing Mom and Dad in Spokane, I waited for them to pick up.

"Are you in Nairobi?" they quickly asked.

"No, no," I replied. "I'm here in Kigali."

I had a lump in my throat as I leaned against the wall and slid down to the floor beneath the window. It was 5 a.m. on their forty-fourth wedding anniversary, and they didn't seem to mind that I had forgotten. We had a wonderful visit, and though I can't remember much of the conversation, I do remember their mentioning that they were planning on spending their anniversary in Coeur d'Alene, Idaho. I also remember how moving it was to hear their voices.

## Another Neighbor Killed

The longer we stayed in town, the more uneasy I began to feel. I sensed that something was not right at home and knew we needed to get back as quickly as possible. We had only been gone four hours, but it seemed like many days since the Interahamwe had pushed us out of the ditch that morning.

By this time the road leading into our neighborhood was completely dry and free of any slippery patches. Wanting to settle our bill for the push out of the ditch, I stopped and asked around for the little old man we had agreed to give payment to. No one could find him, so we asked the people there to send him to our house when he turned up.

When we arrived safely at home, we were greeted with both miraculous and terrible news. Mrs. Seraya explained that an hour and a half after we left, Anitha had gone outside to get some water from the small swimming pool in the front yard. Some soldiers saw her through the gaps in the gate and said, "Hey, come down here and open up the gate!" She quickly went back inside and told Mrs. Seraya about the soldiers calling from the gate. Mrs. Seraya then went down and greeted them.

"Good thing you came," they said. "We were just about to break down this gate. We're checking all the empty houses on this street."

"Well, this house isn't empty," she replied. "We're living here."

"Who's living here?" they demanded.

"The director of ADRA," she said calmly.

"Where is he now?" they continued.

"He's gone to town to get a laissez passé," she patiently explained.

Then they asked how many people were staying in the house and Mrs. Seraya said, "Five."

Several of the soldiers were in front of the gate, and others stood alongside the side fence. Mrs. Seraya felt surrounded as she started back up the driveway and said, "I'm going to get the padlock key."

"Wait, stop!" they called after her. "Don't bother, we're not coming in."

Just as suddenly as they had arrived, the soldiers left and moved on down the street to our neighbor's small adobe brick home to check everyone's ID cards there. One young woman who worked for the family couldn't find hers. Our neighbors later said that she looked and looked, but when she didn't find her ID, they murdered her. It was so senseless—someone's life or death decided by a word written on his or her ID card. Horrible.

Everyone was extremely relieved when we got home. It had been terrifying, particularly for Anitha and Janvier. Mrs. Seraya told us, in no uncertain terms, that both Pastor Seraya and I were never going to leave together again. Janvier quietly turned to me and said, "If it wasn't for the protection of God, we would not be here."

Just before sundown, there was another knock at the gate, and Mrs. Seraya went down to see who was there. After a couple of minutes passed, Pastor Seraya followed his wife outside. Growing restless, I looked out the window and saw a crowd gathering. I knew from past experiences that sometimes my presence complicated things and, since they didn't call for me, I stayed out of sight. I continued trying to raise someone on the radio at the ADRA office in Nairobi. I had promised Teresa that I would let her know when I made it home safely after my first day out of the house.

We all let out a collective sigh of relief when Pastor Seraya and his wife came back into the house. Apparently, the men who had pushed the car out of the ditch had come to collect their money. Because this was not their territory, our neighborhood's local militia wanted to know what they were doing at the gate of "their" missionaries. As was often the case these days, a crowd quickly started to grow. It was good to hear that our local militias were looking out for us, but with the murder of our neighbor earlier in the day, we knew that our safety was never guaranteed. It was extremely difficult to identify what factors determined whether something would escalate into a deadly situation or de-escalate into nothing.

After more time spent on the radio, I finally managed to get hold of someone at the Nairobi ADRA office, and she assured me she would tell Teresa that I had survived my first day out in Kigali. This Kenyan woman was so kind, and at the end of the transmission she said, "Thank you. I want to encourage you for the work that you're doing there."

# Chapter 14

# Dallaire and Doyle Describe the Battle

## Transcript of BBC Report With Doyle and Dallaire, May 7

I have enormous respect and appreciation for Mark Doyle, the BBC reporter who spent so much time in Kigali during the genocide. He lived with the UNAMIR soldiers at Amahoro Stadium in the RPF-held section of the city and spent lots of time at the Red Cross and the Mille Collines Hotel on our side of the city. Although I was at both locations often, we never had a chance to meet. Doyle courageously put himself in harm's way so the rest of the world could see and hear the genocide unfold blow by blow, while it was actually happening.

Below is the transcript of a BBC radio segment I recorded at the time. In it, Doyle interviews Canadian General Roméo Dallaire.

*BBC Announcer: Our correspondent in Kigali, Mark Doyle, has been speaking to the General. First, he went to the roof of the UN building in the city to witness the latest fighting.*

*Doyle: There is fighting going on all over the place. I can see smoke rising from the main government army military base in the foreign embassy area. There's smoke also coming from mortar rounds that are landing towards the center of the city. Toward the east, where the airport is, there appears to be a fight going on between the RPF and the government forces, who hold a big camp just near to the airport, and indeed, south of the city there also seems to be almost constant small arms and machine gun fire taking place. I've got with me here General Roméo Dallaire, who is the United Nations force commander. General, it's very confusing, very frightening. What actually is happening?*

*Dallaire: A considerable amount of offense is actually going on around the city.*

*Doyle: Offensive by whom?*

*Dallaire: So far the offensives have been or nearly always have been* the initiative of the RPF. They have been able to conduct maneuvers, where the government forces have been, more often than not, adjusting and counteracting, either locally or from their heavily defended camps. And there are several camps around the city, and some in the city, like you've indicated; the main one that is in the heart of the city, there is smoke coming from there.

**Doyle**: That's the, that's that camp in the West that we can see there.

**Dallaire**: Yes. Camp Kigali. It's the same camp, in fact, where the Belgique soldiers were killed on the seventh of April. I've got troops, liaison staff, with the 300 or so civilians who are held up at the Mille Collines Hotel.

**Doyle**: Those are, those are the Rwandan refugees who have taken refuge there?

**Dallaire**: Those are refugees or displaced people, I mean; they're not outside the country so they're not really refugees.

**Doyle**: So that's also in the western part of the city. And what are your people saying is happening there?

**Dallaire**: Well, I was to have a meeting with the Minister of Defense, the Minister of Interior, the two chiefs of staff—the gendarmerie and the army—and that got called off because of the intensity of the small arms, machine gun, and indirect fire systems going in that general area. So that's all been stopped. The West End is getting hit by indirect fire and some infantry small arms fire.

**Doyle**: So that's the RPF mounting an offensive against a government stronghold there in the West?

**Dallaire**: Well, there is obviously action going on [pause]; you see the mortar taking off [you can hear two huge explosions in the background] and landing in the RPF headquarters area?

**Doyle**: That was a government mortar landing in the RPF area?

**Dallaire**: Yeah.

**BBC Announcer**: Mark Doyle talking to the UN commander in Rwanda, General Dallaire, amid the latest battle for control of the capital.

# Chapter 15

# **Hand Over Your Workers**

**Logic is Not Always Your Best Friend**

**First Week of May**

Deep booms shook the house all afternoon. At first it sounded like someone was going through the house slamming doors. Then I heard explosions roll through the valley, echoing from one hill to another. The fighting was filled with a steady stream of mortars and bullets whistling through the air, and I was certain that it had been the worst day of the war. Sitting in his cage, Jaquou, our African gray parrot, had begun imitating the noises he heard. His whistle began with a steady high note, and then it slid down an octave, like a mortar flying past into the distance.

This morning we had a near-death encounter orchestrated by a neighbor who lives just a couple houses down the road. I didn't know him well, but I recognized him by face. He had recently started going around our neighborhood in a new military uniform and today showed up at our backyard fence proudly carrying an assault rifle. It's disturbing how putting a gun in someone's hands can change his whole personality. He was with two other men, and all three demanded to see the ID cards of everyone staying in our house.

We went inside and brought back all five ID cards. They hardly looked at mine but spent quite a bit of time looking at the four Rwandan cards. Pastor Seraya's and his wife's cards read "Hutu," but Anitha and Janvier's cards read "Tutsi." They handed back the cards for Pastor and Mrs. Seraya, but kept the other two and said, "We want to talk to these two people."

Obviously they wanted to do more than talk to them. As I look back on it, I find it strange that, in times like these, direct communication wasn't an option; everything was implied or worked around. We knew what they wanted to do to Anitha and Janvier, and they must have known that we knew their true intentions, but no one would come right out and talk directly about the threat on Anitha and Janvier's lives. We knew that we couldn't give our friends up, so Pastor Seraya and I began speaking with them.

"Look, these are just two young people who work for us; they are not causing any trouble," we told them.

"Yes, yes we know," they calmly replied. "We just need to ask them a few questions."

"What kind of questions?" we pressed.

"Just questions," they answered, with their hands on their weapons.

Looking my neighbor in the eye I said, "Listen, you know us. We are your neighbors. I have lived here for four years and there is no one in this house who will cause any trouble."

"Yes, we know you and we don't have any trouble with you. We just need to ask your workers some questions."

It became clear that this was not going to end easily.

"Come now, there must be some arrangement we could make. You are good people. You don't want anything bad to happen," I pleaded.

I think they were beginning to see that we were not going to simply hand them Anitha and Janvier. At different points in the conversation we would excuse ourselves for a few minutes, leave the fence, and go into the house to talk among ourselves before coming back out for more discussion.

Finally they said, "Listen, if it were up to us, we wouldn't be bothering you, but we've been sent here by soldiers down on the road. We can't just go back to them empty-handed."

"Okay, what can we give you to take to them?" we asked.

"Oh, you can think of something good," they said with a smile.

We excused ourselves again and went back into the house. After more discussions inside, we settled on offering them the equivalent of $100.

"Take this," we said, poking the money through the chainlink fence.

"Okay," they said, and they turned and left.

Clutching the fence, with my fingers wrapped around the chain links, I let out a deep breath as they disappeared between the houses. It was over, or at least it was over for that day. Stepping back from the fence, I thought of how easily they could have swung their machetes and sliced their way right into our home. The day could have ended so differently.

Part of me wondered what good would giving them money do when they could just come back the next day for more. But then, logic is not always your best friend in situations like this. As it turned out, the young neighbor in his crisp new military uniform was killed later that night.

# Chapter 16
# Heroic Sacrifices

When rockets land close, the sound is all around; you feel a shaking deep in your core. It's impossible to tell where the rockets are falling; there is no way to know if they're landing to the right or to the left. Soon you stop diving for cover each time you hear an explosion, realizing that you will never hear the one that kills you.

That's what it was like the afternoon I was at our church headquarters, two blocks from Kigali Central Hospital, when the hospital was hit by yet another rocket. Gasigwa, one of my ADRA project managers, and I heard the explosion, felt the deep shaking and didn't flinch, but simply continued doing what needed to be done. Lately I'd been finding that mortars fell more frequently in the late afternoon, so I always tried to get home before 4 p.m.

Earlier that same day I had been in Kigali Central Hospital looking for Colonel Renzaho's social affairs man. When I found him, we traveled together to visit two very different orphanages. I was impressed and happy to meet the courageous directors of each, Marc Vaiter and Damas Gisimba. It wasn't long before we started working very closely together to get food, water, and medicine for their orphans.

Marc, a Frenchman, was among the ten westerners who refused to evacuate when thousands of others did in April. Because he had a large beard and long flowing hair, all the kids in the orphanage called him Yesu. Marc had twelve orphans in his home when the president's plane was shot down, and all of them were either HIV positive or had lost parents to AIDS. During the early part of the genocide a mortar hit Marc's house, but fortunately no one was seriously hurt. He then moved his kids to the basement of St. Michel's Church, and by the end of the genocide the number of orphans under Marc's care grew to over 200.

**Protectors**

Close to a week later, Marc and I were standing in the small yard below St. Michel's Church discussing the challenges he was facing in providing for his growing number of orphans. A politician from one of Rwanda's many political parties walked up and introduced herself.

Much chaos had resulted as several newly formed political parties jockeyed for power. With recent politically motivated assassinations, I had grown leery of politicians and their scheming. When Marc began talking with her, I made my escape, only to find myself intercepted by a young man who appeared to be accompanying the politician. He quietly requested a brief visit, and I somewhat unwillingly agreed.

"Is it true," he asked, "that you are trying to help groups of orphans around the city?"

"Well," I replied, "we don't have much, but we're doing what we can."

"That's good," he said with a smile. "I have a group of people that I'm trying to help, and I was wondering if we could set a time for you to come visit them?"

I was skeptical about what kind of group he was referring to, but his gentle and winsome manner pushed my doubts aside.

"OK, how about tomorrow?" We fixed a time, and he suggested a specific roadblock above the market where we could meet.

The next day I drove with Gasigwa to the designated roadblock and looked for the young man, whom I will call Bernard. I was shocked to see that he was part of the gang manning the roadblock. When he had suggested this meeting point, I thought it was just a landmark, like someone saying, "I'll meet you on the corner of 2nd and Elm." It never crossed my mind that he might be an Interahamwe. He saw us and turned to say a few words to his team before walking our way.

"You can leave your car right where it is; we are just going down the block," he instructed.

Gasigwa and I slowly rolled up our windows, climbed out, and locked the car. We walked one-and-a-half blocks down the street and then turned into a vacant lot on the left. The whole time we were walking, my mind was still concentrating on the guys at the roadblock and wondering what we were getting ourselves into. In the back left-hand corner of the lot, Bernard rapped on a metal door, and we were ushered through the doorway into an open courtyard. I scanned the area and saw about forty people in this 60x60-foot enclosure.

*So this was the group he was helping*, I thought. Right in the middle of the plot was a large 200-liter drum, cut in half and resting on three stones, with a fire under it. Something was bubbling inside, probably lunch for everyone. In the far right-hand corner was a very powerful-smelling outhouse, and in the corner to my left was a stinking heap of garbage. As we walked farther into the courtyard, little kids came up and grabbed my hands. The people couldn't help but stare at this white guy, no doubt wondering where I came from and what I was doing there.

Bernard took me to a door on the left-hand side of the enclosure, and we entered several rooms where people were lying on mattresses. They looked bad, deathly sick. As I stepped back into the courtyard, someone brought a boy over and tilted his head to show me a nasty wound behind his left ear with puss oozing out. He had been hit by a piece of shrapnel. The little guy felt feverish and was nothing but skin and bones, the brightness gone from his eyes. As I looked around this miserable scene, I told Bernard I would do my best to get some powdered milk for the children.

Walking back up the street, Gasigwa and I were no longer concerned about the roadblock gang and Bernard's motives. Instead, our minds were swimming in the sights and smells we had just experienced. We said goodbye, leaving Bernard at the roadblock, and climbed back into our car. With my hand on the ignition key, I looked at Gasigwa and said incredulously, "A lot of those people back there looked like they were Tutsis."

"Oui," he agreed.

I don't know how Gasigwa got his information so fast, but he told me there were several young ladies in that group who had been (how can I say this with the respect and honor that needs to be communicated?) sacrificing their bodies to soldiers in exchange for protection of the families there. It was an unimaginable act of love. I find any effort to put myself in the shoes of the young women, or of their brothers, fathers, mothers, or younger sisters, nearly impossible. What courage, what self-sacrifice, what an amazing demonstration of love!

## A Mother's Choice

The next day we came back and parked by the courtyard. We carried in a couple cases of powdered milk we had managed to buy from thieves. Shortly after our arrival, a woman ran inside, crying and wailing rapid, high-pitched yelps. With her hands on her head, she ran back and forth through the courtyard. Suddenly she stretched her hands out in front of her and ran back through the door toward the street. Of course we followed and watched her quickly kneel down in the middle of the road, pick up a pile of rags and hold them to her chest. Only they weren't rags; it was a little boy, her little boy, and he had just been hit by a car. The Interahamwe sped through the streets of Kigali like wild racecar drivers, and to them her little boy was no more than a bag of garbage. I managed to get the mom to stop running in circles and stand still long enough for me to put my fingers to the boy's thin neck, hoping I would find a pulse. Thankfully, it was there!

"Quickly," I said, "let's get him in the car, and I'll take him to the Red Cross hospital." When those words came out of my mouth, I hadn't even begun to think about the challenges of getting this Tutsi woman and her broken son through all of the roadblocks that were between us and the hospital. All I was thinking about was her crumpled little boy, hoping that his heart wouldn't stop beating.

When I pulled up to the first roadblock, I said, "Open up, quickly, please! I need to get this boy to the Red Cross hospital right away. He was just hit by a car!"

The militias at the different barriers were beginning to know me by now. When they looked in the back seat and saw the bloody child on his mother's lap, they quickly barked orders to move the barrier and let me through. The same sequence played out five more times before we pulled into the parking lot of the Red Cross field hospital. We took the boy into a classroom that had been converted to an exam room and set him on a table. When the Rwandan doctor arrived, I left him to do his work and went looking for Peter, one of the expatriate Red Cross staff members I knew. I was hoping that he might have some blankets to share with me for the orphans. He generously gave me forty.

I was very surprised when I walked back into the room where I had left the broken boy in rags. He was sitting up by himself and curiously watching everyone around him. With so many bandages around his arms, legs, and head, he looked like a miniature mummy.

Finishing his examination of the boy, the doctor looked up and exclaimed, "I can't find any broken bones!"

Without an X-ray machine, and not knowing if the child had suffered internal injuries, he said it would be a good idea to keep the boy for observation. I agreed and asked someone to tell the mother, in Kinyarwanda, that I was going to do some things in town, but I would come back later that afternoon and check on them both.

Arriving back at the Red Cross hospital several hours later, I found the mother and son waiting for me in the parking lot. I wished I had been carrying a camera with me. What a contrast to that earlier scene when she had been wailing frantically after seeing her child struck down by a car! The mom now looked so beautiful and peaceful. She had her bandaged boy on her lap, and they both were eating kernels of cooked corn from a ceramic bowl.

During the genocide, things that seemed so ordinary in normal times, like a mother holding her child, touched something very deep inside of me and made me feel, if only for a few moments, that I was being carried away from the ugliness, pain, and brutality that sometimes threatened to drown me.

One of the Rwandan Red Cross volunteers came up to the mom and said, "You know you don't have to go back to that dangerous courtyard in the city. You could stay here at the Red Cross with others who are looking for protection."

Painfully, the mother replied, "My husband and three other children are back there in that courtyard."

I asked someone to translate the conversation between the mother and the Red Cross volunteer for me. When they told me about the rest of her family, I said, "Ask her the age of her other children."

She said she had a baby she was nursing, another boy about ten years old, and her oldest son, her firstborn. "In fact," she said, "you met my ten-year-old. He was the one with the wound behind his ear, the boy hit by shrapnel."

Wheels began turning in my head, and I said to the translator, "Ask if she would be willing to stay here at the Red Cross if I was able to bring her baby and the wounded ten-year-old. I'm afraid the risks of trying to bring her husband and her oldest son through the barriers would be too great."

The volunteer translated what I had said, and the mother sat quietly for a long moment, thinking hard, then hesitantly she replied, "Yes, I would stay."

When we arrived back at the courtyard, everybody gathered around wanting news about the boy.

"He looks like he's going to be OK," I told the crowd, "but they want to keep him overnight for observation. I've come to get the mother's baby, and where's that little boy who has the wound behind his ear?"

One person found the baby and put her in Gasigwa's arms, while someone else pulled the wounded boy to the front of the crowd. We quickly put them both in the back seat. I didn't look for the father. I didn't know what I would say if I saw him. He no doubt was quietly watching from somewhere in the courtyard.

We had no difficulty getting these two children through the roadblocks, but just before reaching the Red Cross hospital

I suddenly had a strange feeling I might have the wrong baby. I pulled over and said, "Gasigwa, ask the boy if this little baby is his sister."

Gasigwa asked, and the boy shook his head and said "No."

*Oh, great,* I thought, *I've got the wrong bare-bottomed baby!* "Gasigwa, please ask him again."

This time the boy nodded his head and said "Yes."

"Come on, Gasigwa, find out for sure," I said with a chuckle.

After another minute Gasigwa was sure we had the right baby, and we drove on.

When I handed the two children over to their mother at the Red Cross hospital, I made a very deliberate decision to lose track of her and her sons. Later, if anyone asked me where this lady and her children were, I wanted to be able to honestly say that I really didn't know. It would be better that way. Throughout the killing, I did my best to remain an impartial humanitarian worker and not be known as someone who was only helping people with Tutsi ID cards.

Several weeks later, the RPF failed in an attempt to rescue people seeking refuge at the Holy Family Church. The genocidal government retaliated by launching a renewed search for Tutsis in Kigali, and the people living in that courtyard were all murdered. This massacre of families, this horrific tragedy, went completely unnoticed by the rest of the world.

In the wake of this renewed rage that flooded the city, it made no difference that the young women of the courtyard had paid such a high price to protect their families. Everyone was killed, including Bernard, the soft-spoken Interahamwe. He was one of thousands of Hutus who were massacred over the course of the genocide, slaughtered because they stood up against the idea that Rwanda would be a better country without a single Tutsi living there. I'm confident Bernard knew what he was risking before he made his final sacrifice.

When the genocide finally ended and the RPF was securing Kigali, I traveled to several places around the city where the people who had not fled were ordered to assemble for two to three days.

The assembly point populations numbered in the tens of thousands. During this time, the RPF soldiers searched house-to-house for any remnants of the Interahamwe and the genocidal government.

On July 6, 1994, I went looking for Thomas, one of my ADRA colleagues. He was supposed to be in Nyamirambo with the people gathered at the St. Thomas Church and school campus. During the three months of the genocide, Dassan and Gasigwa had helped me secretly supply Thomas with money, hoping that he and several others would survive, and they did. At this assembly point, there were more than 15,000 people, and I wasn't sure how Simeon, our ADRA accountant who was traveling with me by now, would find him.

As I waited in my pickup, a man came to the driver's window and asked, "Do you remember me?"

Squinting my eyes, I looked into his face and said, "Yes, yes, I do, but from where?"

"From that courtyard in town! Remember," he reminded me, "you brought powdered milk to our kids?"

"How could that be?" I replied. "I thought everybody there was killed!"

"Most were," he said with a sad shake of his head. "But do you remember that lady with the little boy who was hit by a car?"

"Yes," I replied.

"Well, I'm taking care of her firstborn son, and I'm wondering if you could take him to his mother. His father was killed."

"I'm so very sorry to hear that," I said. "Yes, I will take the boy. I don't have any idea where his mother is, but I will try to find her."

The boy eagerly climbed in the back of our double-cab pickup with a grin that indicated he was feeling pretty special. When I started the truck, however, he got a frightened look in his eyes, so I asked Simeon to invite him into the back seat.

From St. Thomas, we went to St. Paul's, another assembly point near the Holy Family Church, and a similar thing happened there. A lady came up to me while I was still in the pickup and asked if I remembered her.

I squinted again and said, "Yes, I do! Were you at the courtyard place?"

"Oui," she responded with a smile.

"I'm so glad you survived," I said as I got out and shook her hand. "Hey, maybe you can help me with this little. . . ."

As I turned around to motion to the boy in my back seat, I noticed he was gone! I looked this way and that, wondering, *Where did he go?* Then I saw him run around the front of the truck and throw his arms around the lady I was talking with. It turns out that she was his mom's sister. I couldn't believe it! I asked her if she knew where his mother was.

"Yes, yes!" she excitedly replied. "His mama is looking after a house full of orphans over by the Red Cross hospital."

She described exactly which house, and I asked her to tell the boy to get back in the truck; we were going to find his mother.

We pulled into the driveway next to the house where his mom was living and parked the pickup. As we walked through the yard, his mother came out the back door with a basket of laundry and started walking toward the clothesline. She glanced our way, and when she realized that she was looking at her lost son, she dropped her basket on the grass, ran toward us, and quickly scooped the boy into a huge bear hug. She started to cry, and there was not a dry eye among Simeon, Gasigwa, or myself. What an amazing reunion! This mother had all four of her children now, simply incredible. Equally incredible would be the road of recovery she was now required to navigate, a very challenging road for her and the thousands of other survivors.

Chapter 17

# A Death Threat

On Friday, May 27, long before the end of the genocide, Mrs. Seraya came home shaken to the core and horrified by what she had seen. Four people had been murdered at the intersection down from our house. She had come upon the tragic scene unexpectedly and, as she quickly turned to walk away, someone in the group spotted her and called out, "Hey you, we know the Muzungu[22] you are staying with down the street is hiding Tutsis in his home. You tell him that the next time he comes out we're going to kill him." Understandably, Mrs. Seraya was reluctant to pass the death threat on to me directly, but she did tell her husband, and he told me.

After some discussion, he and I decided it would be best for me to stay in the house and cancel the trip into town we had planned for Saturday. The day dragged by at such a painfully slow pace; it seemed like the sun was standing still. I was less afraid of anyone coming to kill me, but was much more concerned for the people in our house. Anitha and Janvier were the initial reason I had stayed, and their safety was always weighing heavily on my mind. Staying indoors meant that I couldn't visit the orphans around the city, and I knew they were desperate for both food and water.

Whenever I showed up with water at Gisimba Orphanage, the children would form a line at the cement water tank, holding out their little tin cups for that one drink of water that often had to last for two days. While pouring water into the reservoir, I would look into their thirsty faces, and a picture of them was permanently burned into my memory. It was that picture that kept coming up in my mind and was driving me crazy as I sat in my house, held prisoner by a death threat. I knew that every day I stayed home the orphans' situation grew more and more desperate.

Sunday, we decided something had to change, but we couldn't

---

[22] The local term for a white person.

settle on a strategy of how to get out and face the death threat. Mid-morning, there was a rattling of the chain at the gate. I looked out the window and saw a young Interahamwe man with a machine gun standing next to a 4x4 pickup. Walking down the driveway, I called out a greeting and then reached through the bars of the gate and shook his hand.

I said, "What can I do for you?" and he told me he had a letter for me from his uncle.

"Who is your uncle?" I asked.

"Mambo," he replied.

What a relief it was to hear Mambo's name! Mambo was a good friend who was in charge of the garage for the Ministry of Transportation. I unlocked the chain on the gate and invited the young man in. We sat quietly on the porch while I read the letter. For the life of me, I can't remember what the letter was about, but I saw an incredible opportunity in the arrival of this young, armed Interahamwe. The fact that he was driving a stolen CARE International 4x4 pickup indicated that he had a high ranking in the militia's organization.

After reading the letter I said, "Listen, I need to talk to your uncle. Could you take me to him?"

"Sure," he said with confidence.

I told the others in the house that I would be going to town with this young man and would be back in a while. When we went back down onto the street I didn't look around much, just headed straight for the pickup and climbed into the passenger seat. There weren't many questions at the roadblocks, and I didn't make eye contact with anyone. Within a few minutes, I was out of the neighborhood. The ice had been broken. After visiting with Mambo at his office, the young man returned me safely to our home.

It seems the neighborhood Interahamwe who had threatened me must have been thrown off balance by my new "friend" in the 4x4. I never ceased to be amazed by the role relationships played in defusing a crisis.

## Chapter 18
# Sniper Faucet

It was Saturday morning, June 4, and a huge crowd of people were lined up at the one place in Kigali you could get decent water. Wedged in among the crowd were a couple of Red Cross trucks filling their huge water bladders. That water was bound for the growing number of people seeking shelter at the Red Cross hospital and for families in the surrounding neighborhood.

For the last month or so I had been hauling water in 20-liter jerry cans inside my Toyota Corolla. I could haul about 200 liters of water in the car, but of course 200 liters wasn't enough for the number of kids living in the orphanages I was helping. The situation was deadly critical at Gisimba Orphanage because children were dying from dysentery. There was no water to drink. There was no water to keep things clean and stop the spread of diarrhea.

On Friday we had managed to get a big flatbed truck that had belonged to Aide d'Action. The foreigners in the organization had evacuated on April 9 and 10, along with everyone else, and the program had shut down. The local prefecture had taken possession of the truck, and Colonel Renzaho agreed to let us use it that day. We had been using one of the prefecture's drivers and were currently only carrying four barrels, when we could have been carrying twenty.

As I waited patiently in the hot sun to fill up my jerry cans and barrels, someone in the crowd came up to me and said, "Hey, there is a water tap that sometimes works at the deserted office of Cole Chemicals down the street. You could try there."

"And there is not a long line of people there?" I asked.

"Well," the helpful stranger confessed, "at times there is sniper fire around there."

I figured we could at least check it out. So I left our place at the back of the line and drove my Corolla, full of empty jerry cans, down the street in search of the "sniper" faucet, with the flatbed truck lumbering along behind me. Sure enough, when we pulled into the parking lot of the deserted compound, we found a working water faucet with only a few kids filling up their little jugs.

The children swarmed my vehicle, and I asked an older one in French if there were snipers shooting around there.

"Yes," he said, "a few, but it is not so bad. We will help you!"

I gave our truck driver some money, with instructions to go into town and buy more barrels, while I stayed and filled the containers we had. The kids proved to be a great help in the process.

After filling all my jerry cans, I waited and waited and waited, but the driver never came back. I drove to town and looked around the place known as the thieves' market, where he might have bought some barrels, and a few other places, but couldn't find the truck anywhere. *Where was my man?* I headed back to the water faucet at the deserted compound, and, to my relief, our truck pulled into the driveway behind me, loaded full with barrels.

The driver said it had taken a long time to find the barrels. He had bought twelve, but they were oily and grungy on the outside and had some sort of gunk on the inside.

We used scraps of paper and handfuls of sand to clean the outside and were finally able to read their labels. They contained some sort of syrup product for making candy, which was good news because it meant the material in them previously wasn't toxic.

Even though they weren't toxic, we still needed to clean them out so we wouldn't be delivering gunky water to the orphans. I asked the growing crowd of kids, "Does anyone want to help?"

Every hand shot up as they shouted, "Oui, oui!"

So I set up a small assembly line. One of the smaller kids cupped her hands to make a funnel around the three-inch hole in the top of the barrel. Another kid poured some sand into the hole and added water.

"Not too much, pas beaucoup," I told them. "We don't want it to get too heavy."

Looking around the unpaved parking lot, I saw a small mound of dirt and came up with an idea. Putting my hands on the shoulders of two of the biggest children, I instructed them to roll the barrels up the little mound and then let them roll back down, and then up again and back down again. We did it several times together until the sand and water mixture had sloshed all around and loosened the gunk from the inside walls.

I then set up another station and helped two more children pour the gunky sand and water mix out, while the previous two children started the process over with the next barrel in the line. With our system in place, I knew it wouldn't take long to get each barrel cleaned.

Just as we got our system running smoothly, a sudden burst of machine-gun fire hit the metal roof of the warehouse next to us, and we all dove for cover.

Still on the ground, I thought to myself, *No wonder nobody ever comes here for water. This is crazy; we've got to get out of here.*

Not wanting to risk anyone's safety, I started to tell the kids we needed to load up and go.

But one of the older boys said, "No, it's OK, it's quiet now, everybody back to your stations!" Surprisingly, everyone ran back to their stations. What an incredible bunch of kids! Despite having to stop and duck for cover four or five times, we repeated each process until every barrel was clean inside and out.

With the completion of the cleaning operation, I wanted to give the kids something for all their hard work. But I had come empty-handed. Then I remembered a box of high-protein biscuits hidden underneath the seat of the truck. I had gotten it from UN soldiers. They certainly weren't the tastiest, but they were high in protein, and I knew that for hungry kids in the middle of these desperate days they would be a real treat.

I also knew that the water these barrels would carry to the orphans would be an even bigger treat for them. I hoped the fresh water would begin to stop the dysentery that was racing through the orphanage. Any leftover water could be used to wash the stacks and stacks of soiled clothes.

It had been an afternoon of long, hot, dirty work. It could have been miserable, but it was not. I have such great memories because of the kids' can-do attitudes. Their choice to make a game of the work made all the difference in the world.

Chapter 19

# Nyamirambo Rescue Mission

## The Situation, June 11

Bright and early Saturday morning, Gasigwa stood at our front gate, rattling the chains. Traveling was much riskier now, and I figured something really bad must have happened for Gasigwa to return so early after last evening's visit. We both sat down in the living room, where Pastor Seraya joined us. Gasigwa began to explain that today would probably be the day that our friends who were hiding at Nyamirambo church would be slaughtered!

Hiding there was Simeon, our ADRA accountant; Aaron, a religious book translator; and a thin elderly night watchman. Hiding in the home next to the church were a group of women, including Aaron's wife, Louise; his sister Hannah; Simeon's young neighbor who was the sole survivor from her murdered family; and a mother with her child. This woman's husband and 11 other children had been killed. Such staggering losses, so enormous that it seems wrong for me to keep on writing without some sort of respectful pause.

Up to this point, we had been secretly sending money to this group, attempting to improve their situation. The neighborhood surrounding them was nearly impenetrable; it was so vicious, in fact, that even the officials of the genocidal government had trouble moving around there.

Gasigwa was now telling us that the Interahamwe had discovered the ladies the evening before. They would have been killed right then except for the fact that he had given the killers money, and they had backed off. He was sure the Interahamwe would return today and kill everyone.

Pastor Seraya, Gasigwa, and I discussed our options. Trying to relocate these people on our own was out of the question. We agreed we would never make it through the first roadblock without someone being killed. And then there were a dozen other roadblocks separating them from the Mille Collines Hotel. This hotel had been a safe haven under UN protection. Strangely enough, it also served as an exchange point for people who wanted to get into the RPF-held section of the city and other people who wanted to get out of the RPF-held section of the city.

As we considered asking Colonel Renzaho, the man in charge of Kigali, for help, we realized that we couldn't be sure if Renzaho's people would even have any authority in that chaotic part of town. We had no way of predicting how he would react to such a request. Up to this point, I had not asked him to help rescue any Tutsi people. I did my best to give him the impression that my work was strictly involved in emergency relief efforts for orphans. On top of all this, we didn't even know if the recently discovered women were still alive. The Interahamwe could easily have come back during the night and massacred them.

Coming back to the idea of asking for help from Renzaho led us to the possibility that, once he knew there were people hiding at the church, he might say he would help us, but then send someone to make sure they were killed. These people had stayed alive this long by what appeared to be the grace of God; perhaps God's plan to protect them did not include our getting involved? We felt trapped in a deadly dilemma as we prayed together. After the "Amen" I looked to Pastor Seraya for a decision. I was convinced that our chances of being able to help were slim to none.

Thoughtfully the pastor said, "We can't sit by and do NOTHING." Gasigwa added that the people in hiding had asked for the telephone number of Renzaho. He thought that perhaps that was an indication they really did want us to contact the colonel. We considered sending Gasigwa back to the people in hiding to confirm if they wanted us to contact Renzaho, but then that could waste valuable time, and perhaps the people would be killed in the meantime.

As we talked further with Gasigwa, more details emerged. The Interahamwe had actually been there four times already. One time, they even had a vehicle with them, which probably meant our friends had already come very close to having been taken away and killed.

Finally, we decided we would move ahead one step at a time, and the first step would be to contact the UN soldiers. I anticipated their response would be that they couldn't do anything without the government's cooperation, which was true. We reasoned, however, that if at least we had them on board, I could have that piece of the solution in hand for step two–asking for help from Renzaho.

The breakfast Anitha prepared that morning didn't want to go down my throat. It was as if my throat was cramped in knots as I tried to hurry the food down. I kept telling myself things like, *There is no reason to be afraid. There have been many times you have sensed God's presence. Just go for it—this is an opportunity!* But it only felt like a bunch of head talk. What was really in my heart was fear, no feelings of hope or confidence, just raw fear that these people were going to be killed.

Gasigwa and I drove into town without incident. I had taped a picture of the U.S. flag, a page torn from Mindy's history book, in the car's back window. That picture, along with my recently acquired official-looking ADRA stickers[23] on the side of the car, seemed to help at the roadblocks. The killers appeared to be getting a little more accustomed to me with each passing of their post.

We pulled into the Mille Collines Hotel parking lot and walked through the spacious lobby, down the dark hallway toward the rooms where I knew the UN soldiers stayed. I knocked on the first

---

[23] A few days earlier David Syme, regional ADRA Director for French-speaking countries in Africa, courageously risked his life to personally bring us some much-needed items, such as handheld radios, ADRA flags, and signs to mark our house and vehicles. The real purpose for his visit, though, had been to stay with the people in my house for a couple of days while I went out to visit Teresa and the children. When it came right down to my leaving, it was decided that David's taking my place would be too risky, largely because David did not have the relationships and rapport that I did. The solidarity that his visit communicated was a huge morale booster, and the radios and ADRA signs, along with a UN flak jacket he somehow managed to snag for me, proved invaluable.

door, but no one answered, then another door, but still no answer. I knocked on four doors without any response. A cleaning man pointed farther down the hall to where he said there were some Tunisian soldiers. I banged on their door and obviously woke one of them up, as a sleepy face peeked around the door.

"Hey, really sorry to wake you up," I said, "but I desperately need to talk to the soldiers in charge here."

He didn't know where the other UN soldiers were, didn't have a walkie-talkie to ask them where they were, and he didn't have any idea when they would be back.

"Thanks," I whispered, turning back toward the lobby, wondering where to look next.

As I walked into the lobby I spotted a UN soldier from Ghana. What luck! Pastor Seraya had introduced me to this man several weeks before the killing started. I eagerly shook his hand and asked if he had a means of contacting the UN officer in charge at the UNAMIR headquarters in Amahoro. He did have a radio and was just raising it to his mouth to call, when the exact officer I was looking for came strolling through the front door. We greeted each other, and he led everyone back down the dark hallway into one of their rooms, where I began explaining my problem.

After listening patiently, having no doubt heard many stories like this already, he said, "I can't offer you much hope. In fact," he went on, "the government probably won't want to move any people [meaning Tutsis] out of Nyamirambo because as long as there are rumors of Tutsis still there, they hope the RPF will hold back on shelling the area."

Though he wasn't very optimistic, I pushed him a bit and said, "Okay, but if I can get the cooperation of the government, would you work with us?"

"Sure!" he grinned.

**Asking for Lives**
OK, step one complete, now step two. Renzaho was based

several blocks from the Mille Collines. I bounded up the stairs to his second floor office and found an unfamiliar lady there in place of his regular secretary. She said the colonel was busy with somebody else, so I sat down to wait. I'm guessing I looked calm on the outside, but inside I was frantically wondering how I was going to begin this conversation. Though I knew the colonel quite well by now, saying something like, "I need your help to save some Tutsis," still didn't seem like a good start.

The colonel's door opened, and another man walked out. I stood up and greeted Renzaho as he came out, his hand on the doorknob behind him ready to close it. I asked if we could talk and he said yes, then stood there waiting.

"Perhaps we could speak in private?" I nodded toward the room behind him.

"Well," he said hesitantly, "this is where I sleep." Looking back into the room he continued, "OK, come on in."

I closed the door behind me as the colonel took a seat on the other side of a nearby desk. He motioned for me to sit on the chair facing him. I glanced nervously around the room, noticing a mattress in one corner and some cooking pots in another. Sliding the chair closer to his desk, I started to make some small talk about the orphans and other situations he had helped me with. Then I decided to dive right in.

"Sir," I said, "I have a difficult request to make. My ADRA accountant, a very faithful man, is trapped with several other people in Nyamirambo." I told him the militia had been there yesterday, threatening the women for the fourth time. I wasn't sure if they were even still alive. "I'm asking your help to move them to the Mille Collines Hotel," I finished.

The colonel abruptly asked where they were hiding. I slowly responded that they were at Nyamirambo Adventist Church.

"There are people at that church?" he asked, with an edge of irritation. Then he pulled out a piece of paper and started writing.

"Come with me," he said, walking into the secretary's office next door. He asked for his official stamp and put the authoritative mark next to his signature. After handing me the letter he told his secretary to locate a certain Major Emmanuel.

No sooner had he said the man's name than that very major stepped through the door. As the colonel and the major started speaking to each other in Kinyarwanda, I glanced down at the letter in my hand and read that Colonel Renzaho was simply asking the major to accompany the director of ADRA to collect his accountant in Nyamirambo.

I cleared my throat and said, "Excuse me, Sir, but there are seven people that need to be collected."

"Seven!" the colonel repeated. I quickly looked into the face of Major Emmanuel to see if I could read any signs of compassion. My eyes narrowed as this feeling came over me that I had seen this man before. He had a hard, cold face, and I couldn't place him.

The conversation ended, and Major Emmanuel turned and left the office. I quickly thanked Renzaho and then decided to follow the major down the hallway. He went into his office, sat down behind his desk, and didn't move, obviously deep in thought.

Uninvited, I stepped inside and said, "I know what a difficult thing it is that Colonel Renzaho has asked you to do."

He grunted something in reply, and an awkward silence grew even more awkward.

Finally I said, "Major, haven't I seen you somewhere before?"

His lips moved ever so slightly toward what I hoped would be a grin, and he said, "You brought an old man to my house last week."

"Oh, yeah, that's right!" I remembered.

A neighbor down the road from us, near the Bible Society and the American ambassador's house, had brought his 93-year-old father to my house in a wheelbarrow. He had started the half-mile walking, carrying his father piggyback. Then, finding a wheelbarrow to lay the fragile old man in, he came the rest of the way to our home. He was trying to move his dad farther away from the battle line that ran so close to our neighborhood.

When he asked if I would help him move his father just a bit farther down the road, I said, "Of course," and backed my car down the driveway.

After getting this man, who was born before cars were invented, a man who no doubt had experienced enough hardship for several lifetimes, settled in the back seat, we headed down the road. The first barrier was no problem, but at the intersection things started to turn nasty. There was a woman in fatigues examining all of our ID cards, and she spent a long time examining the picture in the old man's ID document. At one point she looked as if she was about to tear it in half. Someone else then barked orders at another neighbor in the back seat; it sounded as if they were telling him to get out, but he wasn't budging.

*Oh no,* I thought, *don't tell me some of these people in my car are Tutsis! Could the old man be a Tutsi?* Evidently he wasn't, because they eventually allowed us to continue.

We arrived at our destination, a home farther down the ridge from our house. A military man lived there, and he was not happy with the arrival of another person, adding to the crowd of frightened people already seeking refuge there.

He and I were standing in the side yard as he told me, "I don't know why these people keep coming here! Don't they know that my position in the military makes me a target? But they just keep bringing more and more people."

On the outside, this man looked very harsh, and he did a great job of sounding harsh, but I knew there had to be some good bones in him somewhere. Why else would people be coming to him for help? He warmed ever so slightly as we made more small talk, and when I left it didn't seem as if he was holding it against me that I had brought him one more mouth to feed.

And now, here I was, standing in the same man's office one week later. Incredible! I wondered how many people he still had seeking refuge at his home.

"Tell me if this will be helpful or not," I said. "I have contacted the UN, and they are willing to cooperate if we need vehicles or anything else from them."

He hemmed and hawed, appearing not to want to make a commitment to cooperate. Finally he told me that he was going out toward Rulibrwa brick factory on the edge of town to get his pickup. He said he would then go check out Nyamirambo Church and talk to the chief of the Interahamwe there. We were to meet back at his office around three o'clock that afternoon. I thanked him, shook his hand, and left.

Up to this point Gasigwa had been making himself as inconspicuous as possible in the hallway. I asked him if he'd be willing to go back out to Nyamirambo and tell the people there about this Major Emmanuel.

"Tell them that they need to prepare for something to happen, and if the major shows up, they must trust him," I counseled.

Without hesitation, Gasigwa left on foot. I remember looking down at his very worn dress shoes and wondering how many miles he had hiked, crisscrossing Kigali's hills. Of course, the miles were nothing in comparison to negotiating the roadblocks and all the other violence and horror of the city. Nobody will ever really know the hundreds of risks Gasigwa took and the lives he saved; he was a man of rare courage and wisdom, two qualities so desperately needed in those terrible days.

Back at the Mille Collines, I gave an update to the UN soldiers. Because of the difficult roadblocks and the mortars falling quite regularly, we carefully considered every trip; this time I decided not to risk a trip back home to wait and possibly get trapped there. I didn't want to do anything that might jeopardize the operation, so I sat and visited with the UN soldiers in their hotel room.

"Hey," one of them called across the room to me, "I thought Jews and Adventists didn't work on Saturday. What are you doing working today?" He couldn't keep a straight face as he waited for my answer.

I asked, with a smile, what he would do in my place. These UN soldiers really are some of the finest people you could ever hope to work with. They were noticeably touched the day I told them that I prayed for them and the difficult work they were doing.

A few minutes later, when one of them offered me a beer, I said, "No, thanks, I don't drink. But I would like to borrow a pair of binoculars and go up on the roof to check out my home."

They found me a pair, and I climbed the stairway to the hotel roof.

It was easy to spot the three-story home of the first neighbors who were murdered and then turn to the right to where I lived. My heart dropped as I focused on a huge black hole in the middle of our roof! One of those mortars—No!

I lowered the binoculars, rubbed my eyes, and checked my walkie-talkie to see that it was still on. Earlier that day I had talked with Pastor Seraya, so I knew it was working. Surely he would have called, that is if he had had time and was still alive.

As I raised the binoculars back up to my eyes to take another look, there was NO HOLE! Where did that gaping hole in the roof go? Scanning around, I realized I had been looking at a vacant neighbor's house. I slid down to the floor with a huge sigh of relief. Though the day had started out with a lot of rockets, it seemed things were growing a bit quieter.

Back in my UN friends' room, I found a spot to wait it out on the edge of someone's bed. We hadn't been talking very long when in walked my friend Captain Douglas, a major from Zimbabwe. He was wearing a flak jacket, sunglasses, and a black T-shirt that barely contained his massive arms. He looked as if he'd just stepped off a Hollywood movie set. We had become instant friends sometime earlier when he learned that our daughters, Mindy and Lisa, had been born in Zimbabwe.

"Wilkens, how are you doing? *What* are you doing?" he asked. Holding a beer in one hand, he dropped down into a chair and gave me a huge smile. Noticing my empty hand, he said, "What's this? It's not good that your hand is empty. We can't be drinking, and you don't have anything!"

"No, no, it's no problem," I said.

"Oh, yes, it is a problem," he replied. "This is not right! Hang on a second, one of my friends is going to his room to get you something." A minute later, the guy returned with a can of grapefruit juice.

"Here," he said kindly, handing me the juice. I remember how good that juice tasted going down. Back at the house, we were extremely grateful to have water, and occasionally we would splurge for a visitor and add a little Crystal Lite to the water. But the grapefruit juice was fabulous, out of this world!

**Time to Move**

It was nearly two o'clock, and we had the final clearance from UNAMIR headquarters to cooperate with the Rwandan government in a joint rescue operation. My UN friends were getting really excited as three o'clock, the designated launch hour, approached, especially when they heard that Colonel Renzaho was definitely on board. They hoped to piggyback onto this rescue mission and save some of their friends who were also trapped in that part of town.

Eventually I couldn't wait any longer and said, "Even though it's an hour before my appointment with the major, I think I'm going to go early and see if he's back at his office yet. Hopefully there's been no change."

"OK," the soldiers replied. "If we don't hear from you by radio, we will meet you at Renzaho's office at three o'clock."

Walking down the dark hallway, I heard noise coming from the lobby and was surprised as I came around the corner to see a crowd of people carrying blankets and sacks. Sometimes there would be a CNN cameraman or a BBC reporter or some other group in the lobby, but this group was different.

As I looked for a way around the crowd, I stopped suddenly, frozen in my tracks. I started to recognize faces in the crowd! There was Aaron, there was Simeon, and there was Louise! Tears were coming to my eyes as I made out Major Emmanuel on the far side of the group.

I rushed into the crowd, hugging and talking, and finally got to Major Emmanuel. I wanted to hug him as well, but settled on a handshake. It was unbelievable what he had accomplished, unbelievable. He had done it all on his own, without UNAMIR.

I had no words with which to thank the major. I could have sworn that he almost had a smile on his face.

While hotel security was checking the few belongings of these twelve people (yes, twelve, not seven), I hurried back down the hall to the UN rooms and found the guys as I had left them, drinking and talking loudly.

I said, "Hey, you guys won't believe it, but my people are here!"

One of them shouted, "Everybody quiet!" and said, "Say that again."

"I said that my friends are all here; they're out in the lobby. Major Emmanuel brought them here all by himself. By himself."

With that, the soldiers headed for the door as one body, and for a moment the door opening was packed with bodies as they all tried to get out at once. Pouring into the lobby, they couldn't believe their eyes.

"Where is he? Point out Major Emmanuel!" they ordered.

When I did, they all gathered around him, bombarding him with questions. No doubt they were hoping he would simply turn his team around and help them get their friends out of hiding.

In the meantime, I took the group to the top floor of the hotel, which was a bare, vacant restaurant. We sat down on the carpeted floor and had a deeply moving time of prayer. Tears were flowing.

Slowly they started to piece together for me the details of what happened. There were three men and nine women in all. When Major Emmanuel arrived, he found the Interahamwe already in the house, threatening the women.

One of the ladies said to me, "As the major came in, these killers had their machetes already raised up in the air above our heads, and we were on our knees praying!" Honestly, the timing could not have been more dramatic.

The major barked orders at these young thugs to get out. He said, "I'm taking these people!" I can easily imagine they figured he was taking them to abuse and to kill them himself.

Simeon told me that when all twelve of them climbed into the bed of the major's pickup truck, the major's soldiers surrounded them and remained standing. He said he had looked into the soldiers' faces and saw some of the meanest-looking guys he had ever laid eyes on.

This was the first time Simeon and the other two men had been outside in the daylight in over two months. They really didn't know if they were being rescued or being taken somewhere to be slaughtered.

While making the harrowing flight from their homes to the church two months earlier, they had seen horrible sights of slaughter that would be forever etched in their minds. Then, during the weeks of hiding, they listened to terrifying reports on the radio of the killing going on throughout the city and the whole country.

Now they were actually standing huddled together in a pickup bed out on the streets in broad daylight. The journey to the Mille Collines Hotel was a ride of gut-wrenching fear. In order to reach their destination, they would have to go through some of the bloodiest roadblocks in Kigali, which were manned by vicious extremists from the northwest.

On the outer edge of the Nyamirambo suburb, there were four roadblocks that were notorious for their brutal savagery. This day, however, three of them were mysteriously unmanned, and the fourth opened in advance so that the truck didn't even have to stop. It appeared that they were going to miraculously pass through them all without incident. The women had convinced the three men to cover their heads and shoulders with cloths they offered, hoping to pass them off as women.

Just as the road passed above what was known as the "thieves' market," they came to a roadblock where the Interahamwe seemed determined not to let them pass. Simeon told me how Major Emmanuel and the head of the roadblock gang shouted back and forth at each other, and it started looking as if the roadblock gang was getting the upper hand.

Everybody was ordered out of the truck onto the ground. It

was at that point that the three men disguised as women were discovered. The men thought for sure this was where they were going to die, then and there. But Major Emmanuel did not give up, and eventually he managed to get everyone safely back into his truck and through that roadblock.

And now, though they were at the Mille Collines Hotel, they still were not truly safe, but they were a whole lot better off than a few hours before. Fortunately, it wasn't many days before they were "traded" with people from the RPF side of the city and taken to the relative safety of Kabuga in RPF-held territory.

Lying down that night in the hallway of my house, I read Psalm 34, as Teresa and I had promised each other we would do every night. After blowing out the candle, I looked into the blackness above me and thought back over the day.

I'd been concerned about how I could participate in this rescue operation and maintain a low profile if it really did happen. Taking my car, with its ADRA stickers, was out of the question. I finally decided I would wear a baseball cap, sunglasses, and my blue UN flak jacket so as to blend in with the others as much as possible. Gisimba Orphanage was also located in Nyamirambo. If I was to have any hope of continuing to take supplies to those orphans, I couldn't risk being labeled as working with the evacuation of Tutsis. But Major Emmanuel had taken care of everything.

Thinking about those people at the Mille Collines Hotel, the rescued ladies' stories kept running through my mind. They said they had not slept at all Friday night, but had spent the whole night in prayer. When I saw them they looked so worn down, their reservoirs thoroughly depleted. I can't adequately describe how exhausted they appeared, and neither can I explain how impressed I was with them. I know that others in history have gone through much longer times of suffering and deprivation, and the point is not about comparing who suffered longer or more. But those who have suffered and those who have witnessed know something of the admiration I felt for these survivors. They saw their neighbors and families wiped out, and they were nearly killed themselves, but they did not give in to despair. In the way they talked and moved, they radiated gratitude so powerfully.

This Saturday night they were bound to sleep better than they had in a long, long time. It didn't matter that they were on the hard restaurant floor and that it was the top floor of the hotel where no one wanted to stay for fear of mortars. We all had passed through one day we would never forget.

Trying to fall asleep, I thought back to that morning when Pastor Seraya, Gasigwa, and I were huddled in the living room, asking God what to do, and we decided to move ahead step by step, relying on relationships we already had. *Wow,* I thought to myself, *to think that I had almost not dared talk to Colonel Renzaho that morning . . . to think how I doubted that anything could be done that day.* What was it I had thought? *The chances were slim to none.*

## Chapter 20
# Biscuits and a Baby

### Pinned Down in the House

Father's Day, June 19, began with two of our living room windows getting shot out. One bullet penetrated the steel tubing of the window frame and nicked Teresa's piano. We were happy to see that it was coming from a sharp angle to the house and not straight up from the road, meaning that most likely we were not the intended target. Seems we were often caught in the crossfire.

I remember pulling the ham radio out of its hiding place in a suitcase full of Barbie doll clothes. After hooking it up to a car battery and screwing the antenna back in, I flipped it on and called for Tango Whiskey. Faithful as always, she was there, and Shaun was the first person to wish me a happy Father's Day! I missed my family all the time, but especially on days like that Sunday, when the fighting was so intense that I couldn't go out and help the orphans.

Being forced to stay home allowed me the chance to catch up on my tape recordings of what had been happening. My work had been so frantic lately that when I got home I would quickly eat something, collapse on the mattress in the hallway, and fall asleep. I felt guilty that it had been two weeks since I had made any recordings for Teresa.

Later that morning a bomb exploded 100 yards down the road in the direction of Heri's orphanage. Gasigwa and I decided to go outside and make sure everyone was all right. Fortunately, the mortar had landed in an empty lot, and the only casualty was a papaya tree.

The neighborhood was strangely quiet as we walked through it. Families were sitting in their dark homes with the shutters closed, waiting for the gun battle to pass over. As our neighbors saw the two of us walking in the street, heads started popping out of the windows and doorways, and neighbors waved and greeted us.

Suddenly, Gasigwa and I heard bullets and quickly jumped in the ditch.

We moved along cautiously, alternating between the ditch alongside the road and the paths tight up against the walls of our neighbors' houses. Just before we got back to our house, a bullet whizzed by me at body level. You can usually tell if they are high overhead or whistling along at body level, and this one was low. I immediately looked over my shoulder, and Gasigwa was gone!

"Gasigwa!" I shouted, but there was no sign of him.

After a few tense moments, he came running around the corner of another building, with a bullet in his hand. It couldn't have been the same one that just whizzed by, but it was from the assault rifles being used around here. With all the bullets and bombs flying around that day, we still couldn't figure out if the RPF was getting the upper hand or if it was just another day of fighting.

At one point during those weeks, Gasigwa's neighborhood had been overrun by fighting. While most of the forty people who were hiding in his home escaped, some were not so fortunate. I still can't figure out how he had that many people in his tiny home, and I am amazed that Gasigwa himself wasn't killed.

On the day of the attack the Interahamwe tied him up while they killed several of the people who had not escaped. Perhaps he was spared because of his integrity and reputation over the years, for being there when his neighbors needed help. That might explain why forty people fled to his house in the first place.

During the days of hiding, each time the Interahamwe came to his place, Gasigwa would buy them off with a chicken from his chicken project in exchange for the lives of those in his home. They would say, "Yes, we will take the chicken now and come back later to kill the Tutsis." How bizarre: a chicken traded in exchange for a life.

After his neighborhood was decimated by the war between the Rwandan government and the RPF, and everyone had fled from his home, Gasigwa and I managed to get his family moved into the Mille Collines Hotel. We felt it was the safest place for them at that point. Many times during the harrowing trip to the hotel, the family was just a whisper away from being murdered. Gasigwa could have moved into the hotel with his family, but he would not have been able to move freely in and out every day. He would not have been able to help in our efforts to care for the orphans around the city. That's when Gasigwa accepted my invitation to move into our home.

## Feeding Our Neighborhood Kids

A week before Father's Day, I had set up a distribution program where we handed out high-protein biscuits from the UN to orphans living with families in our neighborhood. I started doing it as a result of the increasing level of hassle I was getting at local roadblocks each time I left home.

The militia kept saying, "Why are you going to help orphans in other parts of town when we have orphans all around here?" They couldn't seem to understand that, as bad as it was in our neighborhood, it was even worse in other parts of town. But I knew I needed to help them out, too.

On Friday, June 17, the fighting was raging hot and furious, and I decided that the battle was too fierce to consider taking biscuits to our neighborhood distribution stations that day. Immediately after I made that decision, I heard a banging on our front gate. It was our distribution volunteers from the station below our house, and they had braved the gunfire for their biscuits.

As I walked back up the driveway after giving out several cases, I paused for a moment to search the brick wall by the front door. I was pretty sure that earlier that morning I had heard something slam into the side of the house. Sure enough, buried in one of the bricks was a huge armor-piercing bullet. I couldn't pull it out with my fingers and left it to be dug out with a chisel later. By the end of the genocide I ended up with a sock full of bullets and fragments that had hit or entered our home.

The determination and courage of the distribution team that

had just come by convinced us that we should go ahead and carry biscuits to the other distribution points. We would walk instead of taking the car, since that would have made too big a target.

Dassan, my ADRA colleague, arrived and joined Gasigwa and me. They each hoisted a couple of cases of biscuits up on their heads, and I stacked two on my shoulder. We headed out the gate in the direction of the Pentecostal Church. I was wearing a blue UN flak jacket that David Syme, my ADRA regional boss, had managed to snag for me when he made his gutsy three-day visit to my house less than two weeks earlier. I also had one of the handheld two-way radios in my pocket that he had brought. Being able to communicate with the people in our home when I was away from the house released so much tension.

I chose a path that passed by a small crater in the road, created by a mortar that had exploded there the day before. We had actually been in the church when the deafening shower of dirt clods rained down on the metal roof following the roar of the explosion.

Arriving at the church, we left biscuits with Angelique, our team leader. Before leaving, we checked to see that she and the others had their lists of the orphans and were prepared to carry out the distribution.

Our next and last distribution stop was a Catholic chapel that was located down the ridge from our home. We had gone only about half a kilometer when we met the Rwandan Catholic sister and her team of volunteers from the chapel.

Knowing how bad the fighting was that day, they had taken the initiative to walk toward our house. We all crowded into a little makeshift bomb shelter on the side of the road, a small two-story building under construction. The concrete slab for the second level provided us with a bit of protection from the violence all around us.

As we handed over the biscuits, the Catholic sister started to tell me the story of the gorgeous little baby cradled in her arms. Her father had been killed about a month ago and her mom about a week ago, both of their deaths caused by bombs. The baby was wrapped on the mother's back when she was killed, and her body had shielded the baby from the explosion. A small cut from shrapnel above the baby's eyebrow looked to be healing nicely.

The night before, the younger sister of the baby's mother was also killed. During the previous weeks all of the siblings to this baby had been killed as well, so she really had no family left.[24]

The times were hard for everybody, and the Catholic sister asked me to take the baby to one of the orphanages she knew I worked with. As she held this precious one out to me, I looked into her sweet face, and my heart melted instantly. A huge smile spread across her perfect little face as I said, "Yes, of course I will take her." The healthy little baby looked so alert for a six-month-old. She must have received a whole lot of love before her family was taken from her. Many African babies cry when they see a white person, but this little one wasn't the least bit frightened.

On the way home we kept a low profile by hunching over and following as many narrow paths between mud brick homes as we could find. Walking along, we were greeted with warm smiles and people called out, "Muzungu, where are going with that tiny baby? Komera, Muzungu, Komera," which meant, "Courage, white man, courage."

---

[24] It never crossed my mind whether this baby was Hutu or Tutsi until I started to write this story up. Bombs could very well have killed the parents, or perhaps the bomb story was invented because all the baby's family had been Tutsi and was killed. Fifteen years later, I met up with this little girl and the family who took her in. She was doing wonderfully!

Chapter 21

# Angelique

**Bomb in our Market**

Angelique stepped out into our path as I carried our precious new baby back past her church, and she said, "Give me that baby. I want to keep that baby. I'll just take this baby home with me."

As I handed her the baby, I tried to guess Angelique's age, and figured she must have been about thirty years old. She didn't strike me as the motherly type. Her outgoing personality had made her quite effective as our volunteer team leader for distributing UN food. She also definitely knew the ways of the streets and how to handle crowds. There was no way that I was ready to hand this priceless little girl over to a woman who had been so hardened by life. When I reached for the baby, her little eyes searched my face, and then she stretched her chubby arms toward me.

"Sorry, Angelique, looks like she wants to come home with me," I smiled, as I took her back and waved her little hand toward Angelique. Angelique said something in Kinyarwanda, and after we got a few steps away, out of earshot, I asked Dassan what she had said.

"She said, 'Okay, white man, keep on going with your baby.'"

Back in the house Pastor Seraya asked me with a smile, "Where did you get her?"

"Well, I left with some biscuits and returned with a baby. A fantastic trade, don't you think?" I said, before I told him the story.

Gasigwa had remained at the market near our home to get a haircut, and we weren't back at the house long when another explosion shook every window in the house. With fear in my voice, I said, "Hey, that one sounded like it could have landed close to where we left Gasigwa!"

We were all relieved when Gasigwa showed up a few minutes later, with a solemn look on his face. "That bomb exploded 50 meters away from where I was, and Angelique was injured," he said, out of breath.

"Let's find her and take her to the Red Cross hospital in town," I replied.

We quickly pulled things together, planning to get other things taken care of while in town. But by the time we got through the two roadblocks and reached our neighborhood market, we were told that Angelique had already been taken to a military camp hospital. When I heard this, I knew that if I had left that baby with Angelique, another bomb would have changed her young life yet again.

Since we couldn't do anything for Angelique, we decided to continue to town. I had been feeling bad that the fighting had kept me from taking water to the orphanage. Without a doubt, the last drop there had been used up. We also needed to repair a couple of flat truck tires.

**Botched Rescue Attempt**

Things were really tense in the city center. We were told that the night before, a unit of RPF soldiers, dressed in Rwandan government uniforms, had come stealthily down the valley and up the hill to the Holy Family Church, where hundreds of people were seeking refuge. They had been on a rescue mission, but things didn't go as planned. I don't know how many people were killed in their failed attempt, but a large retaliatory killing against Tutsis followed. As the story unfolded, it all started to fit together. I remembered looking across the hillside at the Holy Family Church that morning, seeing stuff scattered all around the ground, especially to the left of the church. I thought it was a bunch of garbage, but when I got out my binoculars I saw human bodies—too many to count, way too many. I lowered my binoculars with a wretched feeling in my stomach. I didn't want to look again, but I had to, to be sure.

When Dassan arrived at the house that morning, he had confirmed what I had seen through the binoculars, and the townspeople were now supplying more details.

The streets were strangely empty and silent; there was a palpable feeling of unease. Word came over my handheld radio from the UN that the Interahamwe were moving from room to room at the Mille Collines, looking for people to kill.

We immediately thought about Gasigwa's wife and three small children, as well as Simeon, Aaron, Louise and the others who were rescued from Nyamirambo. By the time we got to the hotel, the militia was gone and, miraculously, everyone was all right. I left Gasigwa there so he could spend some time with his family.

Heading back home, I was concerned that the same militia would begin another sweep looking for Tutsis in our neighborhood.

Things around home didn't seem much different, and later that afternoon after Gasigwa got back, we found out that Angelique was back from the military camp and in great pain, so we headed to her house to check on her. When asked if she would like to go to the Red Cross, she whispered a strained "Oui" through exhausted lips. "But let's wait until tomorrow morning."

## Hospital Run

The next morning we got an early start because we had so much to do. First, we needed to deliver Angelique and two other wounded neighbors to the Red Cross hospital. Then we needed to stop at Mille Collines. We were expecting Simeon and the Nyamirambo group in the hotel to move to the other side of town in the UNAMIR/ Red Cross "people exchange program." I was hoping to get to them before they moved. Lastly, we had to take our new baby to Marc Vaiter and his growing community at St. Michel's Church.

We found the Red Cross swamped with casualties. The parking lot was filled with blue tarps, and the tarps were filled with the wounded. Two bombs had landed in the central market that morning; some casualties had been sent here and the others to the Kigali Central Hospital.

I went to look for any familiar staff members. Just outside one of the classroom doors, I came across a little boy sitting on a wooden chair. His friend was kneeling next to him, holding his hand. As I looked closer, my stomach turned. Where his left shin, ankle, and foot should have been, there was nothing, only a flap of skin hanging below his knee. Both of the little boys were being so brave, and I couldn't help but think about soccer and life with one leg, if he even survived. It's always the kids, the ones who have no say, who pay the highest price.

I continued my search and found a familiar nurse who listened patiently as I talked about the people I had brought from my neighborhood. "We'll do our best to get to them once we've gotten through the worst of these," she said, waving her hand toward the parking lot.

So we settled Angelique and the others needing treatment under the shade of a tree and then continued up the hill to the Mille Collines Hotel.

Buses and trucks for the transport mission were pulling into the parking lot as we arrived. I carried the little orphan baby in my arms as we went inside. It was hard, very hard, to let her go, but with the rising tension in our neighborhood, we didn't think it was wise to keep her there.

As we stepped into the lobby of the hotel, the scene was chaotic. Gasigwa's eyes searched everywhere as he began wading through the crowded lobby, looking for his family. He wanted to be sure that they stayed at the hotel, where he felt they would be safest.

Making my way upstairs, I found Simeon's group and gave him some money, not knowing just what they would need and where they would end up. As I came back down into the lobby, I saw cameramen maneuvering through the crowd, angling for the best shots. Instinctively, I avoided the cameras, hoping to keep a low profile. Cameras were flashing all around, and a guy with a TV camera caught up with me as I headed back outside. He asked if he could film me with the baby I was carrying. I mumbled something, but kept on walking toward my car.

"How many babies are in there?" he called after me.

"I don't know," I replied over my shoulder, "and this one is not even from the hotel."

Later, I heard from one of our friends in Belgium that it was announced in her church Saturday morning that I had been killed. She stood up in the middle of church and said, "No, he hasn't. I just saw him on CNN carrying a baby through a crowd at the Mille Collines Hotel."

I drove off, holding the baby on my lap as we navigated the barriers between the hotel and St. Michel's. A mortar had landed on Marc's house sometime earlier, with no injuries, but it made the house unlivable, so he had moved into the church.

When we arrived at the church, an excited group of orphan girls came running up and gathered around, extremely happy to have a new baby in the family. I handed her over to one of the orphanage's volunteers, along with a little bit of baby cereal and formula that we had been using. As I left, I heard the girls arguing over who was going to care for their new baby.

Their visible excitement over the newest addition to their family was in stark contrast to Marc's appearance; he looked so worn down. Ten weeks would wear anyone down, and being with the kids 24/7 was grueling. Driving away, I thought, *It's been a whole lot tougher for him than for me.*

Earlier in the day, a couple of guys from Pharmacists Without Borders showed up on our side of Kigali, and one of the group members, by the name of Michel, wanted me to help him get an appointment with Colonel Renzaho. That afternoon I took him for a visit with the colonel and then back to where some of his other buddies were hanging out at Mille Collines.

It was there that I was introduced to a French diplomat named Bernard Kouchner. He was about to take off on a tour of the city, and one of the UN soldiers assigned to escort him pulled me aside and asked if the orphans were still at Gisimba. I told him they definitely were and told them the best route to take to avoid sniper fire. He asked if I wanted to go along, and I declined, thinking about my wounded neighbors needing to be picked up at the Red Cross.

**Neighborhood Medic**

Turning into the parking lot I saw Angelique, still under the little tree where I had left her. Even though many people had been cleared from the parking lot, there were still others in far worse condition than she was.

I asked a Rwandan nurse I knew if she thought my group would get seen today.

"It's not likely," she said, motioning for me to follow her into their pharmacy. She picked up an empty black garbage bag and started going down the aisles, pitching supplies into it: bandages, rolls of gauze, disinfectant.

"Do you know how to give shots?" she asked. "We don't have many more oral antibiotics, but we have these doses of penicillin that you can inject. I also have some prepared tetanus shot doses you can give as well."

I told her the only shot I had ever given was insulin to a friend when I was a kid.

"Pull up your shirt," she said, getting ready to demonstrate how to give a shot. She pinched some of the skin above my belt between her thumb and index finger and told me, "This is the best place to give a shot, just pull the needle back a little bit after poking it in, to make sure you haven't hit a blood vessel, and then slowly push the plunger."

I walked out with a garbage bag of medical supplies and a "good luck" from this nurse, who either had amazing trust in me or was incredibly desperate—probably the latter.

Loading everyone back in the car, we started for home. Snipers had shot at us quite a few times lately as we drove through the valley leading in and out of our neighborhood. I knew that speeding over the bumps would be painful for Angelique, but considering the alternatives, I felt I had no choice. I pushed the gas pedal to the floor and headed toward the exposed section of the valley.

Angelique started to moan just before a burst of bullets tore into the dirt next to the car. My shirt collar filled with dirt clods, and I remember reaching for the window crank to close my window, even though I thought, *It would be stupid to close the window now.* I tightened my grip on the steering wheel with both hands and shot out of there as fast as my diesel Toyota Corolla would go.

I dropped Angelique and the other neighbors off at their homes and went home to fill a gym bag with some of my new medical supplies. Then I walked back down to Angelique's home to make my first house call.

Pulling open the flattened steel barrel that had been fashioned into a door, I stepped into the dim room, where Angelique lay on a grass mat. She had two serious wounds caused by the bomb shrapnel, one on the top of her left forearm and the other high up on her left thigh.

I decided to start with the forearm. After unwinding the gauze and gently pulling back the pads the soldiers had placed over her arm, I got my first look at the wounds that I would soon become very familiar with. The one on her arm was about six inches long and two inches wide. There was exposed fatty tissue, and when she moved her fingers and hand I could see tendons moving. I wiped it with disinfectant and put on new pads and gauze. *That wasn't too bad,* I thought.

"Okay, now for the upper thigh," I said, as Angelique's mouth formed a slight smile.

There was a pungent smell of urine as I unwound a strip of gauze. I was glad for the rubber gloves the Red Cross had given me, and I had to keep telling myself to keep going, don't stop now.

I was in for a huge surprise, though. There were just a couple of pads over the small wound on the back of her thigh where the piece of shrapnel had entered. *No big deal,* I thought, as I disinfected the site. But when I started to remove the pads covering the exit wound on the front of her thigh, I discovered I was pulling on one very long piece of gauze packed in a deep hole left by the shrapnel. I kept pulling and pulling gauze, like a magician pulling a never-ending scarf from his sleeve. I pulled more than two meters out of a hole you could easily drop three golf balls into.

I had no idea what to do, and questions started to fill my mind:

Was I supposed to stuff the hole full again? Pulling gauze out was one thing, but could I bring myself to stuff new gauze back in? And what about the pain for her? Doing *anything* to her would have to hurt! Was I supposed to let the hole fill with her own fluids?

I excused myself, stepped out of her little tin-roofed mud brick home into the fresh air of the courtyard, took a deep breath, and felt slightly better.

I pulled the handheld radio from my flak jacket pocket and called, "Red Cross this is ADRA-1, Red Cross this is ADRA-1. Over."

"This is Red Cross, go ahead. Over."

I recognized Gilbert's voice and said, "Gilbert, I've got myself into something way over my head. Is James around?"

"Yeah, he's right next to me. Over." James was a member of one of the teams of expatriate doctors that rotated through every two weeks or so.

"James," I said, "I just pulled more than two meters of gauze out of a wound in my friend's leg. You could easily drop three golf balls in. What am I going to do?"

"Oh, well," he sighed. "Just wrap the leg up and bring her back in."

I bandaged her back up, just covering the top of the exit wound, and put her back in the car. Another painful ride and crossing through what we had now dubbed "The Valley of the Shadow of Death."

At the Red Cross, I found the doctors sitting down for a meal, and they invited me to join them. At first I thought that I should probably go do something in town. However, after thinking about it, I accepted their offer, knowing that Angelique would probably be more comfortable stretched across the back seat of my car than sitting on the ground with the line of people who were waiting outside.

After we were done eating, Eric, another MSF doctor, gave me a hand putting her on a stretcher, and we carried her inside. He saw the bandage around her leg, and I described how I had disinfected the hole and covered it. He said, "Well, you can take her back; that was the best thing to do."

"But, but . . ." I stuttered.

"Do you want me to look at it?" he asked.

"Yes, I would feel so much better!"

As we peered into the hole together, I said, "That white thing in there, is that the bone?"

"Nah," he said, "that's just another muscle." He bandaged her back up and gave her the tetanus shot I had brought back with us.

But when he was about to give her the penicillin shot, he said, "Here, you give it to her. You'll need to give her another one this evening." As I gave her the shot, Angelique looked at me with a questioning look on her face. I explained to her in French that, even though the doctor was there, I was doing it in front of him to be sure I would do it right when I gave her shots later.

"OK," she said.

We got Angelique back in the car and then drove up to Mille Collines to pick up Gasigwa. I found his wife, Esther, but no Gasigwa. She didn't speak French, and I couldn't speak Kinyarwanda, so I was unable to find out where Gasigwa had gone.

I started looking around for a piece of paper and a pen to write him a note, when I remembered the walkie-talkie in my pocket. I called Pastor Seraya and asked him to translate my message into Kinyarwanda over the walkie-talkie. Esther listened to the transmission, said something in reply, and then finished with, "Aye, murakozi." Pastor Seraya translated that Gasigwa was planning on walking home.

As we headed back down into the valley below our house, for what I hoped would be the last trip of the day, the machine gun fire started again. The last time, there had been just one burst of fire, and then it stopped. I hoped it was because they saw my ADRA flag and realized whom they were shooting at. But this time the firing continued all the way through the valley, and thankfully the shots weren't close because I didn't see any dirt jumping around us. I brought my focus back on the road ahead, with the scream of machine gun fire in my ears and Angelique's groans somewhere in the background.

## Solar Shower

I went to take a shower when I got home, with the usual five liters of water. Then it hit me that I had forgotten to lay my black jugs of water out in the sun to heat. *Why not skip a shower today and save water?* I decided.

With a little time to relax, I talked to Teresa on the radio, and that was the best part of my day. To hear her voice come over the radio worked magic on me. Wayne, from MSF, had loaned her a radio and installed it in her apartment, so now I could talk with her and the kids more regularly. I missed them all so much.

Gasigwa arrived not too long afterwards. Looking down through the bars of the gate, I saw our old Isuzu Trooper parked in the middle of the road. We had brought it from the U.S. four years before.

"Looks like the old boy wants to come home," I said to no one in particular.

Later that evening we finished our second meal of the day. Throughout the genocide we ate two meals a day, some granola in the morning that Anitha made from a huge sack of oats we had bought just before the presidential plane crash, and then in the late afternoon or sometimes late evening we had a plate of lentils or beans and rice. We even got a carrot or tomato from time to time that Mrs. Seraya foraged for us.

As the sun was setting, I remarked to Gasigwa that it was time to give Angelique her shot. While walking to her house, we passed our old Isuzu Trooper, and there were a bunch of guys gathered around its open hood.

I gave it a loving pat as we went by and said, "I used to own this car."

Several of the guys in the gang looked up questioningly, and one said to the others, "Where did this car come from?"

"No, don't worry," I said with a smile. "I sold it about a year ago. It's not mine anymore. What seems to be the problem?"

"Something electrical. We think the owner pulled the coil wire before he left, hoping it wouldn't be stolen," one of them volunteered.

"Oh, electrical problems," I said, holding up both hands in mock despair. "Good luck!" They were laughing as I walked away. Neighborhood relations had definitely improved since starting the protein biscuit distribution program.

We called out greetings as we entered Angelique's courtyard and were invited inside. I gave her another shot, along with instructions on how to take some oral antibiotics I would leave with her. We prayed together, just as we did the Friday she was hit. That first time, I had asked several people who were gathered around her if they wanted us to pray. "Oh, yes, please do," they said. I was a little surprised at their eagerness but didn't think much more about it until the day after the genocide ended.

## Chapter 22
# Triphine's Eyes

I arrived at Gisimba Orphanage with medicines for Triphine, the orphanage nurse. I didn't know that she had been taken and killed two days earlier.

"Where is Triphine?" I asked the first person I saw.

They looked down at their feet and wouldn't answer me. I asked somebody else the same question and got the same response. I remember thinking, *My French isn't that bad. What's going on?*

And then it finally dawned on me that she was gone. I had never imagined that Triphine could be killed. It might sound strange, but she was such a core part of the orphanage that I just never thought about losing her, much less whether she was Hutu or Tutsi.

Triphine was kidnapped from the orphanage on the same Friday as the Holy Family Church massacre,[25] and her kidnapping dealt a huge blow to the orphanage. Even though Triphine was the only medical person at the orphanage and had been there for many years, she was more than just a nurse. Her positive spirit and demeanor brought hope and courage to those children when they needed it most. She had, undoubtedly, forged deep and intimate bonds with the pre-genocide orphans, and I'm sure that the children who came to the orphanage during the genocide made instant connections with her. Triphine's loss seemed incomprehensible, both to me and everyone else at the orphanage.

Ten years after the genocide, I finally learned what happened to Triphine. I was told that, during the genocide, the Interahamwe in the area would often bring their wounded to her for medical treatment. I could not understand how Triphine could treat the people responsible for turning the children she comforted at night into orphans.

How did she do it? How could she stand to touch their skin,

---

[25] I was told that the massacre of so many people at the church was the Interahamwe's retaliatory response to the RPF's unsuccessful rescue attempt a day earlier.

to breathe the air contaminated by their stinking drunken breath? How could she bear to disinfect and bandage the wounds that these murderers sustained while committing their filthy acts? Answers to questions like these are sometimes years in coming, if they come at all.

On the day she was taken, the militia arrived and demanded her help in treating one of their wounded men. As they ordered her inside their vehicle, her husband looked out from his hiding place in the orphanage and caught a glimpse of her climbing into the back of their truck. A few of her own children watched her drive away as well, and that was the last time anyone at the orphanage saw her alive. No one at the orphanage knew how she was killed; only her killers knew that. Only her killers knew what the last precious moments of her life were like.

As I write about Triphine, I think that it's very possible that she did what she did because she was forced to. But knowing her for the few short weeks that I did, and seeing the compassion in her eyes, I think she went beyond simply forced acts of medical treatment. I think she saw those killers differently than most of us did, and I think the secret was in the way she looked at people. Perhaps that's what enabled Triphine to care for both the killers and their victims. Perhaps she saw those young militiamen in the same way she saw the children at the orphanage for so many years, as if they were her own. I'm jealous. I want to see the way she did. I want her eyes.

## Chapter 23

# **The Doctor's Dump Truck**

It became apparent that using the prefecture's truck wasn't going to work. There were too many people who wanted to do too many different things with it. Part of the day we used the truck to haul water to the orphanage; the other part of the day the Interahamwe used the truck to haul their stolen goods around the city. I have no doubt they used it for their killing horrors as well, so I wanted to find another vehicle. I went looking for Colonel Renzaho and found him in his office.

"Sir," I said, "I'm really in trouble for a vehicle to haul water for the orphans. Do you have any other resources? Isn't there some way you can help me out?"

"I'm stretched to the limit and don't have another vehicle I can help you with; I just don't have anything else," he replied.

I looked out the second story window of his office, down toward the parking lot, and my eyes landed on a big Mercedes dump truck that had been sitting there for weeks.

"What about that dump truck?" I asked.

"It's not working," he said slowly, as if trying to remember something about the truck. "Someone left it here, asking us to keep it safe. But," he said after a moment's thought, "times are desperate. I know it doesn't have a battery, but if you can get it running, you can use it."

"No problem!" I said as my eyes widened and the wheels in my head began turning. I quickly recalled the group of thieves I had gotten my last battery from, and now getting another one would be just as easy.

"Merci, merci beaucoup!" I said, giving the Colonel a firm,

two-handed handshake. I quickly left his office before he could change his mind. As I went out, his secretary gave me documents authorizing me to use the vehicle for ADRA purposes, which would come in handy when I encountered roadblocks.

The truck had a Mercedes diesel engine that I was not very familiar with, so I went to my friend Mambo, who was in charge of the government garage, and asked for a diesel mechanic. He loaned me one of his employees and together we went to a car parts place one of my Indian friends had owned. Now an Interahamwe was selling the stock out the back door. We bought a huge, long truck battery and returned to the dump truck.

In less than twenty minutes the mechanic had crossed a few wires and the beast roared to life, although it still had its problems. When the clutch was pushed down, the pedal stayed on the floor until you pulled it up with your toe, at which point it had to be pulled up quickly or it would lurch forward and stall. But we soon got a technique figured out to compensate for that and now had a truck that could haul all twenty of our water barrels.

When we got the truck running that first day, a Monday, it was getting late, so we quickly got a couple of barrels of water to Heri's orphanage and our home. While Gasigwa unloaded the water, I went next door, changed Angelique's bandage dressings, and then called it a day.

A few days later, a lieutenant stopped me along the road and asked accusingly where we got the truck from.

"Colonel Renzaho gave it to me," I said. "Here's the letter he signed."

After looking the letter over, he handed it back and said, "Do you know whom this truck belongs to?"

"I believe it belongs to the doctor's family of our late president," I replied.

"That's right," he said, softening a bit, "I know the family."

"Well," I said, "if you can contact the family and we could work out a reasonable price, perhaps we could purchase it from them."

He seemed to like this idea and said he would get in touch

with the family.[26] I told him not to worry about the truck and that we would take good care of it. The truck proved to be a lifesaver in terms of hauling water during the remaining two weeks of the genocide. Of course, at the time I got it, I had no idea there were only two weeks left. An added benefit was that the truck had 100 liters of diesel in its tank when we got it!

---

[26] After the genocide ended, I left Rwanda to take a vacation with my family, and ADRA continued to use the truck. Some members of the family that owned the truck eventually came to ADRA to reclaim it and presented ADRA with a hefty bill for rental fees! Truth be known, if I had not had that truck in my driveway on the day that the city was taken over by the RPF, it no doubt would have gone to Zaire with the fleeing genocidal government.

Chapter 24

# The Massacre is Stopped

### Bullet Hole in My Headrest, June 28

We had planned on getting an early start Tuesday morning, but the fighting was so heavy that we decided to stick around the house until things calmed down a bit. Leaving later wasn't all that bad because it gave us enough time to check out the alternator and sort out some of the issues with the dump truck's air brakes.

When we felt it was safe to leave, Gasigwa drove off with the dump truck and sixteen empty barrels, headed toward the water source. From my bedroom window I had a clear view of the valley, and I watched the truck fly through the terrain and over the rough dirt road, with the barrels dancing wildly in the back. It was a relief not to hear any gunfire.

As Gasigwa began climbing the hill on the other side of the valley, one of the barrels tumbled out the back of the dump truck. We had removed the tailgate, as it was too difficult to load and unload with it on. *Those barrels are like gold,* I thought. *I'm going to have to get right down there and get it before someone else does.*

I put on my UN flak jacket, grabbed my radio and a couple of the UN biscuits for breakfast, and headed out the door. As I sped through the valley, machine-gun fire started ripping up the air. I slid down in my seat, keeping my eyes glued to the road ahead. Then I saw the barrel in the ditch to the left.

Pulling as close to the ditch as I dared, I stopped and, for some reason, felt impressed to reach over to my left and unlock the passenger door. I pulled on the trunk release lever till I heard the click, climbed out, and walked around the back of the car.

Just as I bent over to pick up the barrel, a burst of shots rang out. I plastered myself against the bank and watched as a bullet shattered my back window.

Waiting a few moments in case there was more gunfire, I decided to forget the barrel and started snaking my way along the ditch to the front passenger door that I had unlocked a few moments earlier. I quickly slipped inside and slithered over the center console. Slouching to the point that I could barely see through the steering wheel, I spun out of there as fast as that little Toyota could go.

When I was completely clear of the valley, I pulled over and started picking the pieces of broken glass out of the car. A group of kids gathered around, and two young men helped me pull out the remaining glass. That's when I discovered a bullet hole in my headrest.

"Oh, so sorry, so sorry for you," one of the boys said, as he peeled the broken glass off the sticky paper from my insurance sticker and my license registration sticker. A few minutes later I found Gasigwa at the water source, and he was as shaken up as I was about the close call.

While we were filling the remaining barrels, several people approached me and said, "We're so sorry you got shot at. Courage, don't give up!" It was touching to see the deep concern of these strangers gathered around us. (As I write these words, I wonder if it's possible that these same people were involved in killing.)

As we were filling the last barrel, I said to Gasigwa, "You go ahead toward Gisimba Orphanage. I'll drive up to see Marc Vaiter at his orphanage, and I'll pick up some powdered milk, high-protein biscuits, and sardines for the kids at Gisimba."

We had gotten this food from Pharmacists Without Borders and World Food Program. Marc's orphanage, in the basement of St. Michel's Church, was serving as one of my storage/distribution depots. The neighborhood where the Gisimba Orphanage was located was extremely violent. We knew that if we took too much food there it would be robbed, whereas St. Michel's was in a lower-risk neighborhood.

Since Marc's orphanage was close to Colonel Renzaho's office, I decided to stop by and ask for a policeman to ride along with me. I don't remember having asked for a policeman before, but for some reason that day I thought of it. Perhaps having my window shot out made me a little more cautious. The colonel was out of town, but I managed to get a commune policeman. Though it delayed me, I figured it might just be worthwhile. Before the day ended, it proved to be a very, very worthwhile decision.

I caught up with Gasigwa, who was moving slowly with his heavy load, and we traveled on together. There were no major problems going through the barriers; in fact, to the contrary, we had some pretty warm greetings that must have been the result of my asking Renzaho to get the Interahamwe to back off.

Not long before this, I had stumbled into a meeting or rally of Interahamwe leaders in Renzaho's parking lot. They parted like the Red Sea as I walked through. I felt quite vulnerable and hoped they would not hear my heart pounding wildly away in my chest. Up in Renzaho's office I looked out the window overlooking the parking lot and said, "I don't know what influence you have over these men, sir, but they sure are making my work difficult!" That's all I said, and he did not respond, but I noticed a marked reduction in roadblock hassle after that.

### Three-Hour Standoff

We arrived at Gisimba Orphanage, and Gasigwa drove the

truck up on the bank above the rainwater reservoir to siphon the water out of the barrels. Damas, the orphanage director, was not there, but his younger brother, Jean-Francois, met me in the parking lot.

After greetings he said, "Your coming today is like an answer to prayer. It has been especially terrible here for the last two days. Seven of the people among those hiding here were killed."

He went on to say that there were also between thirty and forty widows who had come to the orphanage to take refuge with their children and that these women were especially at a high risk of rape and eventual murder. The militia had sent a message that this coming night would be their last night. They would kill Damas and his brother and then they would kill everybody else in the orphanage. Tutsi, Hutu, it didn't matter—anyone hiding there would be killed.

Though the people at the orphanage lived under constant threat of death, the tone in Jean-Francois' voice left no doubt that he was sure that this was more than a threat; it was going to happen. Damas had left earlier that morning to try and find help. He didn't know what steps they could take to prevent this threatened massacre, but he had to try something.

As Jean-François desperately continued to explain the situation, fifty young militiamen with assault rifles began to materialize around the perimeter of the orphanage. Most of them were wearing either a military fatigue jacket or military pants. They wore bandanas marked with the well-known colors of the CDR[27] political party, the extremist party that was behind the genocide. They were the hardcore Interahamwe.

When they saw me, they paused. I don't know if it was the handheld radio that I was holding up to my mouth or if it was just the fact that I was a foreigner, but they didn't continue coming straight in. Instead, they moved toward the perimeter to stand with the others. Some of them made a weak attempt at hiding, while others stood up straight and defiant, as if they were sentinels holding their position.

---

[27] Coalition for the Defense of the Republic.

Two or three minutes later, a dark green Mercedes station wagon came ripping into the parking lot. Out of the vehicle stepped the local councilor, in full military uniform. He was the man who ran the local militia as his own private army.

This wasn't my first time meeting him. I had hunted him down weeks earlier in an attempt to recover one of our ADRA trucks that his gang had stolen. They were using it in their work of extermination.

He didn't look very happy to see me this day, but I walked up to him and reached out my hand to greet him.

"It's good to see you again," I lied. "We have a situation here that could definitely use your help."

I know it sounds ridiculous to ask this guy for help when he is the one commanding these killers. He was most likely the mastermind behind the massacre planned for that night. But I acted toward him as I had toward so many other vicious people during the genocide. I tried to approach and treat him like a decent, respectable person. That was my strategy for improving the chances of getting a decent and respectable response.

I didn't get one this time though. He brushed me off and went straight for Jean-Francois. After raging angrily in Kinyarwanda for several minutes, he climbed in his car and took off in a cloud of dust. I asked Jean-François what he had said.

"They are looking for my older brother. They're angry that he's not here, and he said that 'certain people' must leave the orphanage," John-François summarized. He looked beat, completely exhausted, and he probably hadn't slept deeply in weeks.

I can only guess that the militia leader wanted me to leave, along with any Tutsis hiding inside. The militia stayed put, surrounding the orphanage, making sure no one could escape.

It was strange that they neither left nor moved in on us. It had to have something to do with my presence, yet in the early days of the genocide there were stories of militia killing right in front of foreigners so that they would leave the country.

A definite standoff was developing. Every fifteen minutes or so, the councilor would drive past; once I even saw him walking by on the road above the orphanage, looking to see if I was still there.

Gasigwa was unloading water on the other side of the building from me, so I sent a message with one of the orphan boys, telling Gasigwa to siphon as slowly as possible. I didn't know why the militia was not coming in while we were there, but we were going to drag out this job as long as possible. I was hanging on to the hope that something would change and rescue us from the slaughter that loomed all around.

The commune policeman was keeping a very low profile throughout the whole thing. In fact, at one point I thought he had disappeared altogether. He was a smart guy, and he saw the situation we were in. He could have quietly slipped away, or joined the militia, or he could stand with me against the militia. The last option didn't have very good odds of his surviving; in fact, they were terrible. I have to give him credit; although he had disappeared for a few minutes, he came back and stuck around.

I called Mama Papa Zero, the humanitarian unit for UNAMIR, on my handheld radio. "Hey guys," I said, "I'm in big trouble here at Gisimba Orphanage. Big, big trouble! Seven people were killed here last night, and right now we are surrounded by the Interahamwe. They all have assault rifles and are going to massacre us. Over."

Mama Papa Zero responded with the news that they had pulled most of their soldiers out of our side of the city, the genocidal government-controlled section of Kigali, and there were only a small number of UN soldiers left at the Mille Collines Hotel.[28] This

---

[28] Up to this point, a significant number of UN soldiers were at the Mille Collines Hotel, and a few were at the Holy Family Church a few blocks away. Their presence at the hotel was the basis of the security there, and they were also facilitating the movement of people who wanted to get into the RPF-controlled section of Rwanda. Of course not many of the people who wanted to reach the RPF-controlled zones were able to get to the Mille Collines Hotel, but those who did were exchanged with people in the RPF zone (mostly people who fled to Amahoro Stadium next to UNAMIR HQ) who wanted to reach the genocidal government-controlled zone we were in. In the end, there were still people at the Mille Collines Hotel who feared to be in either zone of Rwanda, so they just stayed put.

was the first I had heard of their departure, and I was hit with a sense of doom, fearing a massacre would happen now that they were no longer there.

I called the Red Cross on my radio and was very glad to get Philippe Gaillard, the head of the Red Cross, on the radio. After explaining our situation to him, he said he would send a call for help to Colonel Renzaho's office and another one to the gendarmerie (the Rwandan police force). A call for help from the police was sketchy at best since sometimes the police participated in murdering and sometimes didn't.

Thanking Philippe, I added that the Interahamwe were looking for Damas. Philippe responded, "He's right here in my office."

"Great!" I replied. "Don't let him come back here. They're looking to kill him."

I'm not sure how much time had passed by this point. It's hard to judge time when at any moment you think you may be killed.

Gasigwa finally finished emptying all of the barrels. It was hard for Gasigwa to do anything slowly since he goes through life with such energy and determination, but he did manage to stretch this job out.

I sent him off to the gendarme camp with instructions to tell them what was happening here. It seemed best to keep the commune policeman with me. At one point, I told him the people of the orphanage were preparing some tea for us. Then, after we had some tea, I lied to him, saying that we were waiting for the orphanage director to return. We just sat tight for quite a while, maybe two hours; I'm not really sure. I know I prayed a lot, reciting Psalm 34 quietly in my mind and asking God, *Is this it?*

During the waiting, I saw the councilor appear every now and then, while the rest of the gang hung around like a pack of wolves. After what seemed like an eternity, a double-cab pickup drove into the parking lot with seven red-bereted gendarmes. I don't know how to describe how relieved I was to see them!

The lieutenant stepped out of the vehicle and surveyed the situation as any police officer would. One of the first things he said was, "We've got to get some of these people in the orphanage moved tonight!"

It was good to have what I hoped would be an ally, someone able to make decisions. I asked if he and his men would spend the night at the orphanage, and he shook his head *no,* saying, "There are just way too many militia. Listen, you go back to the gendarme camp and tell my captain we have to have more help here."

Immediately Jean-Francois pleaded, "No, don't go! If you go, they will kill us! Please, please don't go!"

I looked at Jean-François and then back at the lieutenant. I looked into the lieutenant's eyes and asked myself if I could trust him. Up to this point I had only had positive encounters with the police during the genocide. They had helped me retrieve a stolen car at one point, and another time I stumbled upon them in a standoff with the Interahamwe that ended with a lot of shots being fired into the air. My impressions were that there was no lost love between the two groups.

But if I choose to leave, would it really be only to save my own skin? What if I left and, as soon as I pulled out of the parking lot, I heard gunfire explode behind me? Would the lieutenant join with the militia in carrying out a massacre? As I said earlier, some gendarmes were known to kill.

Jean-François continued to plead, "No, don't go! If you go, they will kill us! Please, please don't go!"

It was one of the hardest decisions I had to make during the whole genocide. I was sick to my stomach and felt like vomiting. Finally, I decided to trust the lieutenant. I had been waiting for something to change in this certain-death situation, and I felt convinced that this lieutenant was that change, that opportunity we had been waiting for.

"Jean-Francois," I said, "listen to me. I'm going to go find help. If I don't find help, I will come back!"

It felt as if I were offering him very little to hang on to. I felt terrible as I opened my car door and climbed in, taking the commune policeman with me. It felt as if I were abandoning everyone at the orphanage. I didn't feel there was any *right* choice.

It was incredibly tense as I pulled out of the parking lot and up to the first barrier. I was not as concerned with the Interahamwe killing me at the barrier as I was that I might hear gunfire behind me, indicating the beginning of a massacre. Fortunately, all was quiet. Going through all the barriers to get back to the gendarme camp at the center of town was relatively easy.

Upon arrival at the police camp, I hurried out of my car and literally ran from building to building, pushing doors open in an effort to find somebody in what appeared to be a deserted compound. I finally found one gendarme who located the captain.

The captain took one look at me and said, "Wilkens, what are you still doing here in Rwanda?" He reminded me (not that I could forget) how we first met a year or two earlier, when the police sent a helicopter to look for me and a couple of missionary kids when we didn't return on time from a river trip. I was relieved to find someone I knew and could trust, but I had to cut through the friendly talk for fear that the massacre had already started.

"Please listen, Captain, it's urgent! The Interahamwe are surrounding the Gisimba Orphanage, in Nyamirambo, and I don't know if the people are still alive. Your lieutenant told me to come ask for reinforcements," I explained.

"That was you out there?" he asked. "I'm sorry, but I sent everyone I had."

I forced myself to sit down while he made several phone calls. He told me he had another plan if these calls didn't bring about anything. I waited while he cranked on an old military-type telephone, but he didn't find any help there either.

Finally he said, "Wilkens, you go home. I will do the best I can."

"No," I replied, "I can't go home. I promised Jean-François I would find help, or I would go back there myself. Thank you for what you're doing, and please don't stop!"

Before I left the captain's office, he made it very clear that I should not go back to the orphanage that day.

"To go there with water or food is fine," the captain said, "but to go out there to get in the middle of a fight will seriously compromise your ability to continue humanitarian work. Then ADRA will be seen as an agitator."

I thanked him again, got in my car, and made a beeline straight to Colonel Renzaho's office. I was so focused on getting there that I don't even remember passing through barriers, but I know they must have been there.

Even though Renzaho was out of town, his assistant, "the Burgermeister," was supposed to be around. When I got there, they said he was in, but he was eating and could not be disturbed.

Frustrating though it was, I decided not to barge in and went instead a couple of blocks down the street to St. Michel's, looking for Gasigwa. He was there, delivering fourteen barrels of water for Marc Vaiter's orphans. I gave them an update and returned to Renzaho's office to talk with the Burgermeister.

### Asking the Genocidal Prime Minister

Back at Renzaho's office I learned that a special visitor had arrived, Prime Minister Kambanda. The real prime minister, Madame Agathe Uwilingiyimana, had been assassinated on the second day of the genocide, and Kambanda was put in her place. He was one of the top three people orchestrating the genocide. He normally operated out of a city sixty kilometers away called Gitarama, which the genocidal government had relocated to because of the heavy fighting in Kigali.

I explained about the impending massacre at Gisimba Orphanage to one of the secretaries who normally helped me. Then I said rather sarcastically, "Maybe I should talk to the prime minster about it."

"Yes," she agreed, "that would be excellent!"

I couldn't believe what she had just said. *Ask Kambanda for help?* That would be absurd! *Ask one of the guys who was in charge of the genocide to stop a massacre?*

Incredulously I asked, "How do you suggest I do that?"

"Just wait until he comes out of the office down the hall," she said curtly. "You will see two bodyguards on either side of the door."

With huge questions colliding inside my head, I thanked her and stepped out into the hallway. At the end of the hall were the two bodyguards, just as she had said. Finding a chair, I sat down to wait, and soon a soldier with gold-rimmed glasses approached me and asked if I was the director of ADRA. I said I was, and we shook hands before he walked down the hallway to the two bodyguards. I could hear him telling them in French (he must have been speaking in French for my benefit) several good things about the work of ADRA.

Each passing minute seemed like an eternity. I couldn't stop thinking about what might be happening at the orphanage. About fifteen minutes later the door opened, the bodyguards snapped to attention, and out came Kambanda and his entourage. He was quite unique in appearance, with a long beard, crisp military uniform, and a hat that looked like the one we always see Castro wearing. As he walked down the hallway, I stood up and could see that I instantly had everyone's attention.

Stepping forward, I said, "Hello, Mr. Prime Minister. My name is Carl Wilkens, and I am the director of ADRA."

Kambanda stopped, which caused everyone else to stop. He replied, "Yes, I know who you are and about your work. Thank you for the work you have been doing." The soldier with the gold-rimmed glasses said a few more things to Kambanda about ADRA, and then Kambanda turned back toward me and asked how my work was going.

I figured that was my cue to make my case, and I told him very directly, "Mr. Prime Minister, I am coming from Gisimba Orphanage, and it is surrounded by militia. I'm afraid there is going to be a massacre there, if one hasn't happened already." I just blurted it all out and stood there waiting. Then I added, "They all had assault rifles."

"No, no," he said. "Everything's going to be all right there. We are aware of the situation." He then looked at the Burgermeister, who was beside him. "And the Burgermeister will see to it that everybody is OK."

I didn't know what to say or what to do. This was not what I had expected. I suddenly became conscious of my dirty hands as I reached out to shake his hand again. I thanked him very much, and in the middle of the handshake, someone snapped a picture. I stepped back, and the group swished on by. Leaning against the wall in a bit of a stunned trance, I wondered what to do next.

When I stepped back inside the secretary's office, she eagerly asked me how things had gone. I told her what happened, and she said, "Good, good, that's wonderful!" I thanked her for her advice and left.

I paused for a moment when I got back out in the fresh air and thought about my second toughest decision of the day. Should I go back out to the orphanage and tell them of Kambanda's promise, or should I follow the counsel of the police captain and not return to the orphanage that day? I knew I had to trust God, but what action should go along with that trust? I couldn't find a clear answer to that question.

In the end I decided to go home. I stopped by Marc's orphanage, found Gasigwa, and he climbed into that big dump truck and followed my little Toyota back toward our neighborhood. We had to find an alternate route through at least part of the valley because I didn't want to drive the same stretch where my window had been shot out that morning.

The last stretch of the valley was exposed, and shots started echoing all around as we came out on this dangerous piece of road. I pushed the gas pedal to the floor, causing my car to fishtail wildly, narrowly missing a huge hole in the road next to a log bridge. Gasigwa's big truck clumsily hurried along behind me. When we parked our vehicles in our driveway, we were both surprised not to find one bullet hole.

Though we were dead tired, we still needed to go down the

road and change the bandages on Angelique. Her arm was looking pretty good, the hole in her leg did not smell quite as bad, and she didn't have a fever.

As I was walking back home past Heri's orphanage, he came out and greeted me.

He was all smiles as he said, "Everybody in the neighborhood is so happy that you are home safely tonight. We heard that your car was shot, and somebody was even saying you had been shot in the leg. Everybody has been asking, "What has happened to our Muzungu?""

Another neighbor came out before I reached our house, and he wanted me to turn completely around so that he could see for himself that I wasn't shot anywhere. Concern from our neighbors was encouraging. It seemed that the tide of some of the earlier frustration and anger was turning, probably due to the fact that I was treating Angelique's wounds. They saw how I came to her house every night to change her bandages.

As I lay down on my mattress in the hall that night, the fate of Gisimba Orphanage was still very heavy on my heart.

## Chapter 25
# Dallaire and the UN Pickup

There are no words to describe the depth of relief and gratitude I felt after arriving at Gisimba Orphanage the day after the thwarted massacre. We found that everyone had survived the night! Obviously, Prime Minister Kambanda had done what he said he would do and stopped the massacre.

Gasigwa and I arrived late in the afternoon with more water and food loaded into our "new" UN pickup truck. Though we were relieved for the moment, we knew things were far from good. A lasting solution for the orphans' security still escaped us, so we decided to carry on until we found something better.

During this time we never knew what would happen from one day to the next. The way we got our hands on this "new" UN pickup is just one example.

It was a very sad-looking little double-cab pickup parked in the Mille Collines Hotel parking lot. The front fender was bashed in, the back window busted out, and a ponytail of ripped-loose wires hung beneath the ignition switch. You could barely make out the bold black UN letters on the door because the whole truck was smeared bumper to bumper with mud and grease. That was the Interahamwe way of applying a "natural" camouflage coating. Many vehicles had been stolen from the UN, and this was one the UN had evidently recovered and now appeared to have abandoned. At least that's what Dassan and Gasigwa were telling me as they urged me to ask the UN to give it to us.

The beat-up truck had been sitting in the same parking space for several weeks, and every time we drove past it, my two faithful, hardworking colleagues were pressing me to ask "my friends" at the UN to give it to us.

I said, "You guys have no idea how much red tape would be involved in asking the UN for this truck, and in the end, they would never give it to us anyway, never."

But Gasigwa and Dassan would not give up, so I finally gave in to their pleas to contact Mama Papa Zero. "OK, OK, I'll ask," I said, "but you'll see, there is no way they will give it to us."

When I talked to my Canadian friends over the radio, they said, "Sorry, there is a policy that states that no non-governmental organization can use UN vehicles." That was exactly what I expected. "But," the UN transportation officer continued, "General Dallaire could make an exception to this policy."

My eyebrows rose as I said, "Really?"

"Yes," he replied, "but the general is in a meeting right now, so I'll have to wait until he gets out. Here at Mama Papa Zero we do have a pretty direct line to him, but I can't promise anything. A rule is a rule, yet the fact that you can get into Nyamirambo neighborhood with aid and we can't should be worth something," he concluded. I thanked him and we signed off.

The next morning I got a radio call from Mama Papa Zero, and they said the truck was ours to use! We covered the UN letters with ADRA stickers, attached an ADRA flag, and were ready to go after figuring out how to hot-wire it.

I threw some sardines, cornmeal, cooking oil, and five empty water barrels in the pickup that same day and headed out toward Gisimba Orphanage, hoping against hope that they were all still alive. On the way, we stopped at a water point that I had rarely used because of the danger of stray bullets that regularly whizzed through the air there. Today, however, things were a bit calmer, plus I was in a hurry, so I decided to take the risk. We pulled up and stopped at the water station behind a couple of other vehicles.

With Gasigwa at the wheel, I sat down on top of an empty barrel and waited for him to move forward under the hanging fire hose. My radio crackled a message, but the volume was so low that all I could hear was "Mama Papa Zero, nothing heard, over and out."

Pulling the radio out of my UN flak jacket, I turned the volume up and called, "This is ADRA-1 calling Mama Papa Zero, do you copy? Over."

"Good copy, ADRA-1," they said. "We want to confirm that the vehicle you got from us was a Toyota 4-Runner. Over."

"No," I replied, "it's a Nissan double-cab pickup. Over."

They didn't seem to hear me because the next thing I heard was "Fox Trot Niner something something. Over."

As I tried to figure out what they had just said, Gasigwa pulled the truck forward under the three-inch fire hose. I grabbed the hose, pushed it into the small opening of the first barrel, and nodded for someone to flip the valve open. I should have been holding it with two hands because the thing kicked wildly with the high water pressure and started spraying water everywhere.

I dropped the UN radio in the mud and shouted for someone to turn the water off while I jumped out of the truck bed to retrieve my muddy radio. As I bent down, the radio I used for home communication fell from my pocket into the mud, right next to the first radio. I quickly wiped both of them off and said,

"Hey, Mama Papa Zero, are you still there? I just dropped you in the mud!"

"Yes, we copy you. Fox Trot Niner would like to talk with you. Over."

"I'm not understanding you very well," I replied, "but I want to tell you how much I appreciate this truck. In fact, I'm using it right now to haul water to the orphans. Now, what did you say, something about 'Fox Trot Niner'? Who is that? Over."

"Fox Trot Niner is the Force Commander, and if you don't have anything else to do right now, he would like to talk to you. OVER!"

I could hear the guys at Mama Papa Zero chuckling.

"Oh, sure, yes, put him on, please. Over."

Then a clear, strong voice came over the radio.

"Carl, this is Fox Trot Niner, General Dallaire. How are you doing out there? Over."

"Very good, Sir, very good! And thank you so much for the truck, Sir! Over."

"That's no problem, Carl. We know you're doing good work,

and if there's anything else you need, please let us know, and, if things get too hot, don't hesitate to call on us to get you out of there! Do you understand? Over."

"Well, OK, Sir. And thank you so much for this UN walkie-talkie, Sir. Over."

"Yes, you keep us informed on your activities so we can know how to best be of assistance. Over and out."

Just that quickly, the radio conversation ended, but it was a definite boost to my day. Though I had no intention of calling on them to evacuate me, it was nice to have the offer. They had come to my home twice already, offering and then insisting on evacuation, and I was glad that they didn't hold my earlier refusals against me. The next time I would talk with General Dallaire would be in his office at the end of the genocide, when he greeted me with, "Wilkens, come in my office. How the hell did you do what you did?"

Well, we did what we did one day at a time, and this day our hearts were overflowing with gratitude when we found that the orphanage was safe for another day.

2005 Reunion With Damas and His Wife at Gisimba Orphanage

## Chapter 26

# Killers Volunteer

### Walking to Town, July 1

Three days earlier, as we drove home on the evening of the near-massacre at Gisimba Orphanage, snipers opened fire on us. We were in the valley below our house, and the shots came from our right. As the road bent to the left, it felt good to have the heavy steel bed of the dump truck between the shooters and us. The sun was just setting, and I clearly remember seeing bluish puffs just ahead of the truck as the bullets tore into the dirt road.

The next day, I decided to leave the dump truck at the house until the snipers moved on. This was the day we got word we could use the abandoned UN pickup. With the fighting growing consistently heavier on all roads out of our neighborhood, we decided that walking would be safest. This meant we would walk down through the valley and part way up the next hill to the Red Cross. Knowing that it was one of the safest places in the city, we decided that the Red Cross parking lot would be the new parking place for the pickup.

Two mornings later, as we walked through the valley, I asked some kids who were collecting surface water if the shooting was very bad this day.

"It's bad," they responded. "You should not walk on the path in the open spaces. Run low in the ditches over there," they pointed, "until you get to the buildings on the other side." Once we reached those buildings, they said, the snipers would not be such a worry.

From the Red Cross parking lot, we drove to Holy Family Church, where I hoped to find Father Wenceslas Munyeshyaka. I did a double take the first time I saw him, dressed in a black clerical shirt, white collar, and blue jeans, with a pistol shoved in his belt.[29] While discussing the needs of the children taking refuge at the Holy Family Church with Father Munyeshyaka, my handheld radio came alive.

"ADRA-1, this is Mama Papa Zero. Come in ADRA-1."

"Go ahead, Mama Papa Zero, this is ADRA-1. Over."

"We have good news for you. Your orphans have been moved from Gisimba to St. Michel's. How copy?"

"Good! Good copy! Over," I exclaimed with a huge smile on my face.

"We thought you would want to know. Over."

"Thanks so much, I'll head over there now! Over and out."

This was incredible news. The orphans were by no means safe, but by moving from Gisimba to St. Michel's, they were definitely in a much better place. In addition, I was going to have a much easier time taking supplies to them.

As I pulled into the lower driveway at St. Michel's, the place was swarming with people. Everybody was hugging and laughing,

---

[29] Years later, a military tribunal in Rwanda found Wenceslas Munyeshyaka guilty of rape and involvement in the 1994 genocide of the Tutsi and sentenced him in absentia to life in prison. He was found to have delivered hundreds of adults and children to the genocidal militias, who brutally slaughtered them. Following the genocide, he fled to France, and as of April 2011, he was still living there.

and as I surveyed the crowd, I started picking out adult faces I had never seen before. I had no idea that so many adults had been hiding at Gisimba Orphanage.

The practical side of my brain kicked in as I thought, *What is needed in order to take care of this group?* Not seeing any personal effects, I asked one of them, "Where is all your gear, your blankets, and your cooking stuff?"

"They wouldn't let us bring a thing!" was the response. "They showed up with their vehicles and said, 'Everybody! Quick, Quick! Get in the vehicles now! Don't bring anything with you!' So we just came."

They honestly didn't know if they were being rescued or being taken away to be killed. Often trucks would show up at some place of refuge, load everyone up, and take them to the river or some other place and slaughter them.

After further conversation with Damas, the director of Gisimba Orphanage, Gasigwa and I decided to head to the orphanage and bring back anything we could. It got cold at night, and the kids would need their blankets. Also, with so many mouths to feed now, we would need every pot we could get our hands on.

I stopped by Colonel Renzaho's[30] office to thank him for moving the orphans and told him that we needed to retrieve their cooking gear and blankets. He immediately wrote, signed, and stamped a letter authorizing me to collect what I could. I'm not sure why I didn't ask for a policeman this time, but I didn't. Gasigwa and I continued to the orphanage in our UN pickup.

As we pulled into the very familiar driveway, it appeared more

---

[30] On July 14, 2009, Trial Chamber I found Renzaho guilty of genocide, murder, and rape as crimes against humanity, and murder and rape as serious violations of Article 3 common to the Geneva Conventions and of Additional Protocol II. The Trial Chamber sentenced Renzaho to life imprisonment.

On April 1, 2011, the Appeals Chamber of the International Criminal Tribunal for Rwanda reversed two of Tharcisse Renzaho's convictions but affirmed his sentence of imprisonment for the remainder of his life in view of the gravity of the convictions affirmed. (To read more visit: http://relief-web.int/node/394409)

like a ghost town than the buzzing hive of activity we had found on previous visits. Gunfire was popping to the left of the compound, so we went right.

Turning the back corner of the main building, we found ourselves face-to-face with the councilor and his killing gang—the same killers who had been set on massacring everyone here just two days earlier were now caught red-handed, looting the orphanage. Immediately I thought, *This is it. Now I'm going to die over some blankets and cooking pots!*

An awkward silence surrounded us until I remembered the colonel's letter of authorization. Fishing it out of my pocket, I nervously unfolded the note and offered it to the councilor. His eyes moved quickly back and forth through the lines before he said, "Of course, the orphans need their belongings."

Turning, he barked orders to his gang of twelve Interahamwe to help me load my truck! I couldn't believe it as I headed toward the first dorm room with these new "volunteers" in tow. Finding my voice, I instructed them to each lay a blanket on the floor, put as many clothes and other things as possible on it, and tie the corners. I'd give anything for a picture of these guys coming outside with bundles of the orphans' possessions slung over one shoulder and an assault rifle over the other. One of the strangest sights I've ever seen.

It didn't take long to see that our little pickup truck was way too small for our needs, and I asked the volunteers if they knew of a truck in the neighborhood that I could hire. One of them came back a few minutes later and said that they found a guy who was willing to rent his truck to us.

"Great," I said. "Tell him to come. I'll pay him a price that will make him happy."

"No, he says that he wants you to come to his place and make the deal," the militia boy replied.

"Seriously, that's not necessary," I said. "Tell him that he'll be more than satisfied with what I pay him," I replied in my most convincing French.

"No," he said gruffly.

"OK, where is he?" I asked, with a sigh. "Where does he live?"

"Just down the main road, around the curve," the kid explained.

I looked in the direction he pointed and said, "OK, I'll walk down there."

"No!" another guy barked. "Get in the car!" He opened the door of their stolen green Mercedes station wagon.

Getting in that car was the last thing in the world that I wanted to do, but for some reason (maybe it was the gesture with his assault rifle), I climbed in. I still remember very distinctly the sound of that door slamming shut. We drove in the direction the guy had pointed, around the curve, and pulled up in front of a house with a full porch.

*No, not this guy!* I said to myself.

Some weeks earlier, I had stopped for a moment at almost exactly the same spot and let Dassan, one of my ADRA employees, out of the car to make his way deeper into the neighborhood with some money for Thomas, another ADRA employee, who was hiding there. At the agreed-upon rendezvous time I arrived, but Dassan was nowhere in sight. Trying not to look too conspicuous, which was nearly impossible, I casually got out of my car for a look around. The owner of this house we were now parked in front of had walked up to me and gruffly said, "What do you want here?"

"I'm just looking for someone," I explained, while scanning the area.

"This guy?" he asked, holding up Dassan's ID card. My heart sank. I immediately thought they'd killed him. They always took the ID cards of victims before killing them.

I paused and started to rub my forehead, not sure what to say, when I heard Dassan call my name. I snapped around and there, behind some bushes, I saw his head appear!

"They're giving me a hard time here, Mr. Director," he said. My knees felt like they were going to buckle, I was so relieved he was alive.

I can't remember how I eventually got Dassan out of there that day, but now here I was, face-to-face with this same stout man again. He stood there, with a bottle of locally brewed beer in one hand, looking at me through bloodshot eyes.

Clearing the old memories away, I said, "I understand you have a truck I can rent?"

"Oui," he said, between belches.

After a strained conversation, a deal was negotiated to haul two truckloads of blankets and supplies into the center of town. I walked out of the house and told the gang I would just walk back to the orphanage. One of the militia opened the back door of the car and made a motion with his rifle while ordering me to get back in the car. I quickly abandoned my plans to walk and got in the car.

Back at the orphanage, I was mightily relieved to climb out of that car. As the truck pulled into the parking lot behind me, things seemed to somehow change, in very powerful ways. The killers started showing initiative for the job at hand. When I suggested that we stand tables on end on each side of the truck, forming high sides to contain the orphans' belongings, they added their own ideas. As we filled up that truck, an unexpected bond was forming while we worked together to accomplish a common goal.

Years later, I still think back on this event, shake my head, and wonder at the transformative power that acts of service can have on everyone involved. The more the killers engaged their minds and muscles in acts of service, the less I saw them as killers. As I was carrying one end of a table, with an Interahamwe carrying the other, perhaps I too was changing in the mind's eye of this man.

When we got to St. Michel's and started unloading, it was better than any Christmas party I've ever been to. The knotted blankets were untied, and children picked through the pile, saying, "Hey, Joseph, here's your sweater!" and "Beatrice, here's a picture of your sister!" It was incredibly emotional to watch.

Turning from the empty truck, I said to the owner, "I think it's getting a bit late; mortars are falling more frequently. We'll just call it quits with one load."

"Absolutely not!" he scowled. "You hired me for two loads. We're hauling two loads!"

"OK," I said with a ridiculous chuckle. "Let's go get the last load!"

The sun was setting as Gasigwa and I pulled into the Red Cross parking lot that evening. I reached under the dash and pulled out the fuses, hoping to make our hot-wired pickup a little harder for anyone to steal. The thirty-minute hike got us home before it was too dark, and when I walked in the door I said, "You wouldn't believe what happened today!"

Chapter 27

# Snipers

**Young Boy Down**

The morning hikes through the valley were turning out to be not that bad. Each evening we would park our pickup at the Red Cross and then walk back to our house. It took about half an hour. The exercise felt good, though the UN flak jacket got pretty hot at times.

This particular morning near the end of June, Gasigwa and I, along with a neighbor, had made it safely through what was normally the most dangerous part of the valley. Things got crazier just as we were starting over a bridge leading up to the Red Cross neighborhood. Everything had been calm and quiet, and then suddenly bullets began tearing up the air.

"This way!" I shouted, as we scrambled down the embankment away from the gunfire. There were government soldiers at the bottom of the bank, manning a barrier on the road that went under the bridge. They pointed out a path to the left that would be our safest way out of there.

When I climbed into our truck at the Red Cross, I radioed the UN and told them about the sniper fire on the bridge.[31] Up to this point, there had not been much shooting in that area. "Yes," Mama Papa Zero said, "we heard about snipers there, and today we're not driving anywhere near that bridge if we can help it. Thanks for the heads up."

Pulling out of the Red Cross office parking lot, we drove halfway around the block to the entrance of their field hospital. Our first job was to collect my neighbor's wife, who was ready to come home. She had suffered a miscarriage the previous week and continued to bleed for several days. That's when her husband asked for my help to get her to the hospital. As she climbed in the back seat of our

---

[31] This is the same bridge where Captain Mbaye Diagne was killed. He was a UN officer from Senegal who saved so many lives. As he was driving across this bridge, his vehicle was hit by a mortar.

truck, she definitely looked much better than the day when I first saw her.

Two more of our neighbors had also been released from the hospital that day, so the back seat was full as we headed toward our neighborhood. I wouldn't be able to take them all the way home because the snipers in the hills made it too dangerous, but we would take them as close as we could.

People carrying water jugs were walking on both sides of the road as we approached the gas station where we planned to turn right. Suddenly, everyone dropped their containers and started running in all directions. I don't remember hearing any shots, though Gasigwa later said the air was wild with gunfire, but I did see a young boy drop like a rock.

I shouted at Gasigwa, "Stop the truck, STOP right now!" Flying out of the truck, I snatched the back door open and grabbed my neighbor, pulling him with me toward the boy curled up on the side of the road. He was clutching his stomach and crying out in pain. We scooped him up, dashed back across the road, and pitched him onto the laps of the people in the back seat.

Gasigwa made a quick U-turn back toward the Red Cross hospital. Kneeling and facing backwards in the front seat, I reached to where the boy lay and started looking for bleeding or some place I should be applying pressure to. Strangely enough, I couldn't find any blood at all.

At the Red Cross we carried him into a classroom and laid him on a table. The doctor on duty was busy with another patient, so I began checking him more thoroughly. He was still clutching his stomach and crying, but I simply couldn't find where he'd been shot. I turned him over on his stomach, and there was still no blood anywhere. I pulled his shirt up—still nothing—and then started to pull his pants down, and there it was. High on his left butt cheek I finally found the tiny entry wound.

Rolling him back over, I gently but firmly began to pry his hands off his stomach. There was no exit wound. Then I saw a very small bump, like something was pushing his skin up from the inside, just below his belly button. Ever so gently, I pushed the skin down around the bump and was shocked to see the outline of a bullet come into clear view. There was no telling what damage it had caused inside his little body.

When the doctor arrived, I showed him my discovery and then left. I was hoping they would be able to help the little guy, even though they didn't have an X-ray machine or any other diagnostic equipment. I never did find out how it ended for this boy.

## Young Interahamwe

After dropping our neighbors as close to our neighborhood as possible, we ran errands in town and parked the pickup back at the Red Cross just before sunset. Gasigwa had found three cabbages earlier in the day and now walked with them lashed together, balanced on his head. Taking shortcuts through the yards of vacant, western-style homes, we hustled down to the main road close to where the boy had been shot.

As we approached the roadblock by the gas station, I suggested we split up.

"If these guys see that we are traveling together," I told Gasigwa, "it's pretty much a guarantee that they will swipe the cabbages, thinking you have access to more because of me, your Muzungu friend."

Gasigwa agreed, and I went through the roadblock ahead of him without any problem. However, twenty or thirty feet on the other side, a teenager with an assault rifle stepped in front me and poked the sharp tip of his bayonet against my chest.

"Give me money!" he ordered. Even though he was speaking Kinyarwanda, which I didn't understand, I heard the word "amafranga," which means money, and I assumed the rest.

Looking him in the eye for a few seconds, I slowly reached my hand up and gingerly took hold of the blade. I said to him in French, "I don't have any money for you, and there's no way any of us are going to survive these hard times if we don't work together."

The boy kept looking at me as I held the bayonet firmly between my thumb and first two fingers and slowly stepped back from its pressure. I then let go of the blade and started to walk around him. Out of the corner of my eye, I kept a watch on him as he turned, keeping his rifle pointing at me, but I kept on walking. With each step I took, I thought about him pulling the trigger. *How bad would it hurt?* I wondered. Ten steps, fifteen steps. I'd never been shot before. Twenty steps and still nothing happened.

At thirty steps, an older man came out of a house to my right and motioned for me to come to him. I turned slightly in his direction and could see out of the corner of my eye that the boy still had his gun pointed at me.

"How is my son?" the man asked me in French.

"Who is your son?" I responded, still seriously preoccupied with the boy pointing his gun at me.

"He is the boy who was shot just down the road from the gas station this morning. People around here said you are the one who took him to the Red Cross," the father explained.

"Oh, that was *your* son!" I exclaimed. *Wow! What are the chances,* I thought, *that I would be standing right in front of the home of the boy who was shot, while at the same time another boy would be menacingly pointing his weapon at me?* This was an incredible opportunity to drive home the point I had just made about our survival depending on our ability to work together.

Using two of the few words of Kinyarwanda that I knew, I called to the boy with the rifle, "Guino, guino hano," meaning, "Come, come here." He lowered his gun and walked toward us.

"You see this man?" I asked in French. "His son was shot this morning, and I took the boy to the Red Cross. That's what I mean when I say we have to work together if we're ever going to survive these difficult times."

Then, the father of the boy who was shot began to chew out the boy with the gun. I didn't understand the Kinyarwanda, but I sure did understand the finger he was shaking at this boy. And with every shake of his finger, it seemed the boy's head and machine gun were sinking lower and lower. Eventually, the young Interahamwe quietly turned and walked away. The father shook my hand vigorously and thanked me again and again for helping his son, "Murokosi, murokosi cyane!"

About this time, Gasigwa caught up with me, still in possession of his cabbages, and asked what was happening.

"Let's keep walking," I said. "I'll tell you on the way."

# Chapter 28
# How Did it End?

## Go in Your House

For nearly three days the dump truck had been trapped at our home. The last time we had driven the dump truck into our neighborhood, bullets rained down all around us, kicking up dirt and leaving us crouched low in the cab, racing as fast as we could. The sniper activity was definitely on the rise.

While our work of taking assistance to the orphans had been made much easier by the fact that we no longer had to navigate through twenty-plus barriers to reach them, we still couldn't keep up with the water demand. The little UN pickup made multiple runs each day between the water point in the valley and St. Michel's Church, with five barrels each time, but we now had over 600 thirsty orphans, along with approximately 75 adults, who desperately needed more water.

At the end of the day on July 3, Gasigwa and I parked the UN pickup in the Red Cross parking lot and made our thirty-minute trek home. The journey was becoming routine by now. As we rattled the chain on our gate and waited for Pastor Seraya to come let us in, I looked up the driveway at the dump truck imprisoned there.

"Snipers or not, we've got to get this dump truck back in service," I told him.

We decided that, come what may, we would drive out the next morning. We thought it would be best to leave just before sunrise since that was usually a quieter time. If we drove without our headlights on, it might be tougher for the snipers to hit us.

The next morning the alarm woke me out of a sound sleep. We quietly crept out to the truck, where the only things stirring were the morning songbirds. Gasigwa reached for the door handle as I headed down to the gate to unlock the padlock.

The door hinge on the truck screeched frightfully loud as he got in. When he cranked the engine over and that diesel motor roared to life, I flinched and looked over my shoulder, convinced that we had awakened the whole world.

As if on cue, the grating chatter of machine guns filled the air and then—*kaboom, kaboom, kaboom*—explosions shook my chest. These monster guns sounded as if they were right down the road in the middle of the intersection a block away, an intersection we were planning on driving through.

I motioned for Gasigwa to shut the engine down and follow me back into the house. I didn't know if the sound of our engine triggered the gunfire, but the timing sure felt like it.

Once inside, I said, "It doesn't sound good, Gasigwa. If the snipers don't get us in the valley, I bet those guys with the monster guns will fire on us. They will shoot for sure at a truck rolling toward them in the dark with its headlights off. Let's wait a bit and see if things quiet down."

The fighting carried on for over an hour, and when things finally did quiet down around sunrise, I asked Gasigwa to come with me for a look around the neighborhood. As we stepped cautiously out into the street, everything was quiet, ghost-town quiet. I knocked on our neighbor's door to the right; there was no reply. Pushing open the door, we found the place was empty. House after house down the street was empty. I knocked on Heri's gate, and he came right away. I asked if he knew what was up, and he simply said, "Everyone left."

"Oui, it looks that way," I sighed. "I know I don't need to tell you this, Heri, but don't go anywhere" (as if he could go, with 29 little kids). "We will stay in touch; the RPF could arrive anytime," I called over my shoulder.

We went on to the cluster of small buildings, just past Heri's orphanage, to check on Angelique. Her place was empty as well; the only sounds of life were a few snorts from the pigs in the shed to the left. Back at our house we called everyone together to report on what we had found and decided that we should get ready to evacuate in case RPF soldiers came through and ordered us out.

While the others were busy packing inside the house, Gasigwa and I went outside to jump a dead battery on one car and make sure the other vehicles were running. We had just hooked the cables to the dead battery of the Ford when I saw a soldier coming down the hill behind our house.

As he headed toward our fence I asked Gasigwa to go talk to him while I continued to hook things up. I was thinking, *The last thing we need right now is a soldier giving us trouble.*

My head snapped around when I heard the soldier call out in English, "Hey, what are you doing here?" I don't know why I had assumed he was a Rwandan government soldier. His English clearly identified him as an RPF soldier. Many RPF had grown up in Uganda, speaking English as their second language.

Walking to the fence with a surprised look on my face, I introduced Gasigwa and myself. I then told him who else was staying in our home.

"Go inside and remain in your house while we secure the area," he replied. Before acknowledging his instructions and turning to go, I saw a man dash from hiding in a building about forty yards behind the soldier. The soldier quickly turned and in Kinyarwanda he shouted at the man to stop, but the man kept running. The soldier shouted again, but the man still kept running. The soldier fired, and still the man did not stop. After getting hit by six or seven bullets, maybe more, the runner started to crumble. It seemed to be happening in slow motion, and then the soldier turned to us and said quietly, "Go in your house."

### The Babies

Gasigwa and I told Pastor Seraya and the others what had just happened and that we had been ordered to stay inside. I don't think any of us really knew what to think or how to feel. Although we had been hoping and praying for so long that this horrible time would end, we were now hesitant to believe it really might be ending. What would happen to us during and after "the ending," if we survived?

Just how long we waited in our house, I can't say. When we

heard the chain at the gate rattle, I took the key and went down to let two RPF soldiers in. They ordered everyone in our house to come out on the front porch while one of them went in and searched our place. The one who remained on the porch with us didn't appear to be interested in listening as I explained that I was the director of ADRA and was doing humanitarian work in the city.

When they examined everyone's ID cards and saw that Anitha and Janvier were Tutsi, they took them inside for questioning and then brought them both back to the porch. I found out later the soldiers were having a hard time believing that I did not have any guns in the house.

Janvier was instructed to sit down on the cement with his legs straight out in front of him. One of the soldiers reached into Janvier's shirt pocket and pulled out a paper with handwriting on it. He must not have liked what he read because he started shouting loudly at Janvier and then raised his gun over his head, holding it by the barrel as if he was going to use it as a club on Janvier's outstretched legs.

Up to this point I had not interfered with the soldiers' "questioning" methods, but when I saw this guy about to break Janvier's legs, I shouted, "Hey, STOP! I haven't been working to keep this young man alive all this time, only to have you come and kill him now. I want to speak to your commander!" The soldier looked rather startled, and I was hoping he couldn't sense the fear I felt inside.

He slowly lowered his gun and said, "OK, I'll call my commander."

He returned a few minutes later with an officer. After quickly summarizing who I was and why I was there, I said, "Sir, are you aware there is a house full of 29 small orphans just down the street? I'm very concerned for their safety as you secure the neighborhood."

"No," he said, "I don't know about them. Come and show me."

"OK," I said, but then looking at my much-loved friends on the porch the thought hit me, *What if they do something to these people while I'm gone?*

"Sir," I said, "can I have your word these people will be safe?" I held out my open hand in their direction.

"Yes, yes," he said, in a slightly annoyed tone.

Walking down our street with the officer, we came up behind about fifty RPF soldiers with their weapons at the ready, all in a line facing the valley. Several looked back over their shoulders, a bit surprised to see a foreigner. As we approached the orphanage, I was hoping we would only find Heri and his orphans inside.

Several weeks earlier, Heri and I had had a conversation about the day we hoped for, when the RPF would take over the city. I had strongly urged that he try his best not to let any militia hide in the orphanage when that day came.[32] Now, as we knocked on the metal gate and I shouted, "Heri, it's me, open up," I was thinking, *Please no Interahamwe! Please don't let there be any Interahamwe inside.*

Heri came quickly and opened the gate. While introducing him to the officer, I kept looking over his shoulder for any signs of trouble.

Stepping up onto the front porch, the two soldiers with the officer had their automatic weapons at the ready, fingers on the triggers. Sitting in the living room were two women who helped with the care of the orphans.

Heri led the way to a bedroom door, opened it, and stepped aside as the soldiers scanned the room with their rifles. Their faces were quite a sight as they looked down the barrels of their guns into the faces of little ones, quietly standing in their cribs, staring back at the soldiers.

The officer told his men to lower their guns and put on the safeties as we went from room to room, each filled with those precious lives. All these men could do was shake their heads in wonder. After all the horrific, grisly discoveries these RPF men had come across in the aftermath of the Interahamwe's wave of

---

[32] A typical strategy for the Interahamwe would be to get rid of their weapons and try to blend in with the ordinary people.

slaughter, this scene no doubt stood out in stark contrast.

I cannot tell you how proud I was, and am, to be a friend of Heri. The determination, compassion, and bravery shown by Heri, and the women who helped him, had paid off. It was clearly reflected in the well-cared-for children in this home. Heri and his team stand amid the many, many unrecognized heroes of this dark time.

Before the day was over, RPF soldiers had brought powdered milk, sugar, and other food for the children. The service these men provided to the children was just a tiny glimpse of the assistance that would come in the days and months and years ahead, the kind of help that brings healing to a shredded community.


## The RPF Stops the Genocide

It was so quiet that night, and I think the quiet was one of the things that made it hard to sleep. Could it really be over? Could the 88-day-long nightmare have come to an end? July 5th dawned as a new day in Kigali, and in the coming days the liberating light would spread throughout the rest of Rwanda.

The consistent, determined, and disciplined military efforts of the Rwandan Patriotic Front had finally driven the genocidal government out of power and out of the country. It was not the United Nations nor the government of France (which had very close ties with the Rwandan government) that had ended this horror. No other African nation that I know of helped stop the genocide. Thousands of lives were spared because the RPF brought the genocide to an end and eventually brought peace to Rwanda. That will always be huge for me, always.

Throughout history many corrupt governments have committed horrible atrocities and stayed in power for years afterwards, but that would not be the case for the Rwandan genocidal government.

That morning I turned left out of our driveway, unlike the previous three months of turning right. Instead of heading to Colonel Renzaho's office at the prefecture building, I headed toward Amahoro Stadium, where I had arranged to meet with an RPF representative. Mama Papa Zero had helped me set up the meeting at their UNAMIR offices near the stadium.

It was strange to drive into this section of town that had been controlled by the RPF. I had not been here since the killing started. Passing the parliament building on my left, I couldn't miss the gaping holes that pocked its walls, the building's wounds of war.

Showing my ID at the gate, I entered UNAMIR's compound. It was like Grand Central Station. To be in the middle of all this ordered structure and conversation geared toward rebuilding life was a glaring contrast to the past 88 days of ordered violence geared toward wiping out all traces of Tutsi and moderate Hutu lives.[33]

"Meet Major Rose Kabuye, the new Mayor of Kigali," one of the UNAMIR officers said, as I shook hands with a tall, serious-looking woman.

After briefly explaining who I was and what I had been doing since April 6, I offered to provide assistance in hauling water to the thousands of people in Kigali. The RPF had assembled them in several locations around the city, while they swept the rest of town for any remaining resistance.

"If you could just issue me a laissez passé," I concluded, "I could bring water to some of the assembly points."

"Issue you a what?" she asked.

"A laissez passé, a document authorizing me to drive around Kigali to do humanitarian work."

"Why would you need that?" she asked. It was a reasonable question for someone who had not been living under the controlling structure of the previous government.

"Well," I replied, "I'm sure there will be soldiers at the intersections, and a paper with your name and signature on it could facilitate my work."

"OK," she said agreeably, "why don't you write what you think

---

[33] The extermination efforts were so thorough that birth certificates, wedding licenses, property deeds, and other records showing that the targeted people ever existed, were destroyed.

you need, and I will look it over and sign it." Looking around for a pen and paper, I wrote out my own laissez passé, and she signed it. I thanked her, said I was looking forward to meeting her again, and left.

The Red Cross provided Gasigwa and me with a 4,000-liter, rubberized canvas water bladder. We loaded it into the back of our dump truck and started taking water to the thirsty men, women, and children around Kigali.

There were many people in the parking lot of the Mille Collines Hotel as we entered. We were driving slowly through them when a girl's voice called out to me, "Monsieur le Directeur, Monsieur le Directeur!" It was Chantelle, one of our neighborhood kids, making her way toward us. Gasigwa stopped as I leaned out the window to greet her. "Monsieur le Directeur," she said again, out of breath, "Angelique is here, and she needs her bandages changed."

Smiling, I said, "So good to see that you and Angelique are safe here. I'm sure that there are some real doctors here now that are able to care for Angelique."

While emptying our load of water, I saw two young men and thought, *I know those faces, but from where?* On the trip home, it came to me. I hit the steering wheel and said, "I know where I've seen those two guys before! They were part of the group who came to our fence demanding that we hand over Anitha and Janvier."

Back at the house I said to Anitha, "Hey, I just saw two of the guys at the Mille Collines Hotel who wanted to kill you and Janvier."

I don't know what I expected her to say, but she was quiet for a moment and only said, "Oh."

"Do you want us to try and find them again and hand them over to the authorities?" I asked, feeling a bit awkward.

A quiet "No" was her only response. It dawned on me that I was more focused on justice than on how Anitha was feeling. There is so much to gain from learning how survivors survive "life after genocide." The world needs more, so much more, to be written about this incredible process.[34]

## Angelique's List

The following days were filled with times of joyous reunions and heart-crushing discoveries of friends lost. We all survived by focusing on what we had, not what we lost. It was such a relief to drive around without fear of mortars, snipers, and especially the threat of the Interahamwe.

We drove twenty minutes out of Kigali to Kabuga in the east and found Simeon, our ADRA accountant, and others. When Simeon and I arrived back at my house, I honked for someone to come and unlock the gate. Waiting there, it was so satisfying to look around and see that our neighborhood was filling up as people were released from the assembly points.

Then I caught sight of Angelique's mother walking down the road toward us. She was a cute little old lady, and I got out and gave her the traditional Rwandan greeting. I held onto her hand with both of mine as I asked in English how she and her family were. Simeon translated for me because she only spoke Kinyarwanda. She withdrew her hand from mine and lowered her head as she quietly said, "Angelique yapfuye."

"Angelique is dead," Simeon translated very simply. I had recognized the Kinyarwanda word for dead, but my mind refused to put that word together with Angelique's name.

"Wait a minute, Simeon, double-check," I asked him. "I was at the Mille Collines Hotel the other day and Chantelle said Angelique was there and needed her dressings changed."

Simeon spoke again with Angelique's mother, and it was confirmed that, yes, Angelique was dead. I expressed condolences to her, and she turned and left.

As Simeon and I went into the house, he asked me to tell him

---

[34] Though there is little written about how the survivors are coping after the genocide, progress in recording survivor testimony is being made. You can learn more at this website: http://voicesofrwanda.org/

more about Angelique. I briefly described her and what I knew of her story. He looked at me and shook his head. "This woman is famous in this part of Kigali. She was responsible for compiling the list of those to be killed in this area. She is responsible for the deaths of many."

I was staggered by this news; this was not the Angelique we knew! But as I sat down trying to process this, memories of several incidents started taking shape in my mind. One memory was how I had noticed that when I showed up at her home in the evenings to change her dressings, she often had many visitors there, some in military uniform and some not. By itself, this was not out of the ordinary; in Rwanda, visiting is a huge part of life. But another memory was how amazingly well-informed she was about the fighting that was going on all around, though at the time I didn't think much of it.

Then one particular memory came back to me—it was now crystal clear in my mind. This incident happened sometime before we set up our high-protein biscuit distribution program, where Angelique was a volunteer team leader. It happened the day a man brought his 90-year-old father to my house in a wheelbarrow, and I took him to Major Emmanuel's home.

On the way there, in fact, almost right in front of Angelique's home, there was an angry gang at the roadblock, and a woman in fatigues had nearly ripped the old man's ID card in half. Now I remembered so clearly the face of that woman: it had been Angelique. I don't know why I had never put this together before, and the more I think about it, I'm glad I didn't. Angelique, the volunteer, was Angelique, the Interahamwe. If I had known what she had done, who she really was, how would I have treated her and her wounds? Would I have helped change her dressings those two weeks before the genocide ended? Then I thought about how we had prayed together several times in her home and how the Interahamwe's attitude in our neighborhood had softened toward me. Whoa. . . .

**Nairobi Airport**

I regret not making any tape recordings of the radio conversations I had with Teresa and the children during the week before leaving Rwanda. That week was an overload of the sensational, good and bad, and I only have a few memories. But the flight out of Rwanda to reunite with Teresa, Mindy, Lisa, and Shaun in Nairobi—that is something I remember very clearly and will never forget.

About half a dozen of us civilians entered a C-130 military transport plane. The entrance was through a huge drop-down tailgate door at the back. The opening was big so that they could drive vehicles through. They were loading some cargo at the time.

The plane was operated by the Canadian military, and it was going to be my first time in a military plane. Someone pointed toward a seat against the left wall of the plane. It was a surreal feeling as I pulled the shoulder straps around me, fastening my back securely to the side of the plane. *Was I really on my way to my family? Was this really happening to me?*

While watching the male and female members of the flight crew go through all their pre-flight checks, I was struck by their attention to detail. They moved with such precision; a seamless flow was happening all around the plane simultaneously as the team functioned as just that: a team. The time of organized murder that I had just lived through stood in stark contrast to these well-organized soldiers who were working together for a common good. A sense of peace was settling over me as I relaxed into the routine of their world, where everything was done so deliberately and thoroughly for the good of others.

Shortly after takeoff, that peace and security was quickly snatched away when I discovered the pilots were still under orders to fly using "tactical measures." In short, it meant that they were required to fly hugging the contours of Rwanda's thousand hills with what seemed like less than 100 feet of altitude cushioning us. One moment my stomach was in my feet, feeling like a thousand pounds compressing me, and then I felt weightless, with the seat harness barely holding my heart from popping out my mouth. I felt smashed, then weightless, then smashed, then weightless.

I was about to throw up when we reached Tanzanian airspace, and the plane climbed to a very welcome cruising altitude. For the rest of the flight I had one thing on my mind: wrapping my arms around my family.

As we touched down in Nairobi I craned my neck around, trying to look out the tiny window and see where we might stop. I hoped immigration and customs wouldn't take too long. I was so excited to see my family that I was about to explode.

One of the soldiers opened a small door on the side of the aircraft, with drop-down steps, and we all climbed out. Then I saw them, and they looked like a dream or a mirage on the tarmac. My Teresa, my Mindy, my Lisa, and my Shaun were all standing 100 feet away!

Words fail to capture all the emotions that were swirling around in my heart and the hearts of the four people who mean more to me than anyone else in the world. For 84 nights I had dreamed of this moment. At times I feared I would not live to experience it, but now here it was.

We ran toward each other and hugged standing up, hugged kneeling down, kissed, laughed, and hugged some more. I didn't want to let go or say goodbye to any of them ever again. As we climbed into the van, I asked Teresa how she had managed to get out there on the runway. "I've made some friends," she said with a smile. The children said, "Dad, let Mom drive. You sit on the bench seat with us!" One on my lap, and one tucked under each arm, this was the way it should always be. Together.

# Epilogue

Teresa and I continued doing humanitarian work in Rwanda until September 1996, when we returned to the United States. It was a great privilege to work in Rwanda after the genocide, alongside survivors and others who worked with such courage, heart, and intelligence to rebuild this treasure of the continent. We are grateful for the wonderful memories made in Rwanda post-genocide. Every year millions of people in Rwanda demonstrate that **nobody is required to be defined by what they lost or what was taken from them, but rather we can be defined by what we do with what remains. In Rwanda there is once again beauty, hope, and forgiveness.**

**What happened to some of the characters in this story:**

**Anitha:** Young lady who lived and worked in our home.

Lost 99 percent of her family in the genocide. She married not long afterward, and they have two handsome sons. Her husband's ID card used to have "Hutu" written in it. Since the genocide, all ethnic designations have been removed from ID cards. She has formed a family, like thousands before her, with one spouse Hutu and one spouse Tutsi.

**Damas Gisimba:** Director of Gisimba Orphanage.

Still running the orphanage.

**Dassan:** ADRA colleague who worked with me during the genocide.

Died tragically in a car accident one year after the genocide.

**Edith:** My mother.

Enjoys retirement, her grandchildren and great-grandchildren, and adopting refugee families.

**Jean-Francois:** Brother of Damas, the Gisimba Orphanage director.

Married with children and very active in the development of Gisimba Orphanage.

**Kambanda:** Genocidal prime minister.

Convicted of genocide and crimes against humanity; serving a life sentence in prison.

**Gasigwa:** ADRA colleague who worked with me during the genocide.

Still working hard every day to keep their three oldest children in college and their youngest in gradeschool.

**Heri:** Ran the orphanage down the street from our home.

Married after the genocide and still working every day to support his family.

**Janvier:** Our young night watchman.

Most of his immediate family survived, hidden by neighbors in Kigali. Following the genocide he joined the RPF and served one year in Darfur with the Rwandan military under UN command, standing up against genocide. He is married with children.

**John:** My father.

Enjoying retirement, his grandchildren and great-grandchildren, and adopting refugee families.

**Marc Vaiter:** Frenchman who remained in Kigali with his orphans.

Continued working with orphans in Kigali for some time and wrote a book in French, *We Couldn't Save Them All*, about the genocide experience. Tragically passed away in West Africa approximately four years after the genocide.

**Pastor and Mrs. Seraya (Foibe):** Stayed with me in our home during the genocide.

They are both enjoying retirement.

**Simeon:** ADRA accountant.

Married with children; still doing humanitarian work.

**Tharcisse Renzaho:** Military colonel, prefect (governor) of Kigali.

Convicted of genocide and crimes against humanity; serving a life sentence in prison.

*The following guides have been prepared by Dr. James G. Brown, professor in the College of Education studies – Chapman University*

# *I'm Not Leaving* - Analysis & Discussion Guide

## Introduction

1. How might an understanding of the genocide in Rwanda develop over time? What elements, sources, or types of information help to develop more meaningful comprehension?

2. What are your reactions to how Wilkens attempts to help others develop an initial understanding of the genocide beyond the staggering numbers (800,000 people brutally murdered in just 100 days in 1994)?

3. What are some of the challenges and dilemmas of studying difficult histories such as the genocide in Rwanda? To what extent do you share any of the ideas noted in the letter by the high school student?

## Chapter 1

1. What might Wilkens have been feeling as he watched his family drive away from their Rwandan home?

2. What was Wilkens' dilemma? What factors might have convinced him to stay or go?

3. Wilkens writes, "Simply being there is often the most powerful factor in making the right decision." What does he mean?

## Chapter 2

1. Wilkens writes that the presence of UN (UNAMIR) forces "… caused people to fall into a false sense of security" (p. 17). To

what extent might the presence of the UN been both beneficial and detrimental?

2. Why might people ignore or minimize the potential danger? To what extent were there reasons to be more optimistic and hopeful?

**Chapter 3**

1. What were some of Wilkens' duties and challenges the first few days as the genocide unfolded in his neighborhood and later in his network of aid workers? To what extent were his actions heroic or simply the work that might be expected given his multiple roles, including father and leader of missionary/aid workers?

2. It is chilling for most who live in more affluent countries to conceive of genocidal acts, especially in their own neighborhood. How might the shock of the violence have affected people both inside and outside Rwanda as the news of the atrocities reached the international community? What might have mitigated the shock and corresponding willingness to respond by economic and militarily powerful Western countries?

**Chapter 4**

1. According to Wilkens, "This family's children play with our children" (p. 23) was a powerful declaration with profound implications. Why was it so impactful? What does it say about the Wilkens and their neighbors?

2. For many, if not all, the decision to stay or go was one-sided. All Americans and most non-Africans (Europeans, Indians, etc.) decided to go. Ironically, Wilkens maintains that it was not a difficult decision for him and his wife Teresa. It was indeed a one-sided decision, but unlike his peers, it was obvious that he would not abandon the Rwandans. What factors influenced his decision? To what extent are these factors crucial in any such significant and life-changing decisions?

3. What might others in the Wilkens family have been thinking when Teresa and Carl made their decision? Wilkens writes, "Teresa was totally with me on the decision... She never once said, "What about me and the children"(p.27)? Often decisions are not as one-sided. What if Teresa, the children, or other family members had insisted on Carl leaving? What did their support suggest about the decision?

4. Which of the following might have been more influential factors in Wilkens' decision to leave or stay?
- Fear for his own personal safety
- His duty as a father and husband
- His sense of duty as ADRA leader
- Orders from the US embassy to leave
- The fact that nearly all Westerners were leaving
- The level of violence
- His religious beliefs
- His connections to Rwandans
- His values and sense of right and wrong
- Support of his family

5. Wilkens writes: "Teresa managed to make life more of an adventure than an ordeal for our children" (p. 37). What might the Wilkens' children have been thinking? They played with their Rwandan peers in the neighborhood where they had lived for several years. They were leaving their home and father behind. What factors might have affected their experiences?

6. As just about all Westerners fled Rwanda, Wilkens recalls thinking "If people of Rwanda ever needed help, now is the time. Instead everybody is leaving." What are some implications of this statement? What were some factors that might have influenced this unilateral and immediate abandonment by individuals, institutions, and governments?

7. Wilkens' decision to stay in Rwanda involved declaring "I have refused the help of the United States Government to leave Rwanda." He writes that the statement "… engraved itself permanently into my memory." How did this declaration change his ideas about being an American? What do you think about the change? To what extent was he a "good American" when he chose to stay in Rwanda? Do you think he still loves his country?

## Chapter 5

1. Wilkens notes that some Rwandans were able to also make the decision to flee or stay. For example, Pastor Seraya and his wife decided to stay and move into the Wilkens' home. To what extent might their motivation to stay and help have been similar to Carl's?

2. To what extent do you agree with Victor Frankl's assertion that even in the grimmest and most inhumane of situations, any person can "…decide what shall become of him – mentally and spiritually?" Or are choices diminished so much that they become meaningless in the face of atrocities? To what extent are we able to remain human in the face of such inhumanity?

## Chapter 6

1. What are your reactions to the BBC accounts?

2. This vivid report was on April 24, two weeks after the genocide began. What does it suggest about what the world knew of the genocide? Could there be any doubt that genocide was occurring?

## Chapter 7

1. Around the second week of the genocide, Wilkens decided to keep a narrative of his experiences by talking on cassette tapes. How might you have recorded your experiences? Why might such recordings be important?

2. What stands out to you about the initial recording of April 19? Try to identify both positive and negative impressions.

3. When Wilkens is questioned by the Hutu soldiers, he says, "This is my country, and I didn't evacuate with the other people because I came here to live with the people no matter what" (p. 43). Why do you think Wilkens responded with these words?

4. Wilkens described the soldiers as "polite and decent." He later wished them courage with their work and as they left he shook their hands as he said good-bye. What are your reactions to Carl's interactions with the Hutu soldiers who were possible perpetrators of genocide? What do such interactions suggest about the complexity of a genocide?

## Chapter 8

1. It is common for people to become bored when they are simply "stuck" or "just sitting around" at home. How is Wilkens' "cabin fever" different from common boredom?

2. Why might Wilkens find Corrie Ten Boom's accounts of the Holocaust to be relevant?

3. Wilkens' early narrative includes this excerpt: "Heavy, heavy fighting all around the house, some big explosions that made the ceiling shake." What does Wilkens do during such helpless times? To what extent would this work for you?

4. What experience leads Wilkens to reach this conclusion: "I've decided I would do well to be slower in forming opinions and faster in looking for the different sides and components of any situation" (p. 49). While this may be important wisdom, why might it also be uncommon?

5. While Wilkens is deeply religious, he notes that "My understanding of God's protection is constantly expanding"

(p. 49). For instance, initially Wilkens and his wife Teresa had concluded that security came from a faith in God. But after a few weeks of living in the midst of a genocide, Wilkens thinks that "God's plan of protection doesn't revolve exclusively around miraculous interventions" (p. 49). Instead, notes Wilkens, "I will experience authentic security when I choose to care for others first instead of expecting to be cared for" (p. 49). What may have caused this change in perspective? What does this say about Wilkens' views of God, his faith, serving others, and the possibility of death?

## Chapter 9

1. Wilkens is again directed to leave Rwanda on April 21, but this time as an ADRA missionary and by the leader of his Seventh-day Adventist church: "This directive is given after much prayer and consultation. It is a decision and not a request" (p. 9). What are the key elements of Wilkens' response to this directive? Should he comply?

2. To whom does Wilkens believe he ultimately answers? What are the implications of this perspective, especially for Wilkens and his actions in Rwanda?

3. Since the genocide began, what conclusions has Wilkens reached about the roles of God and mankind?

4. Where was God during the genocide? To what extent do you agree with Wilkens' suggestion that God was reflected in the actions of the Spanish nuns?

5. What is the connection between faith and choosing to be a more active rescuer? To what extent are people more likely to stand up and respond, rather than stand by and do nothing- when they have stronger moral clarity, such as well-defined and strong religious beliefs?

6. What roles do identity and experience play in becoming an active rescuer? Wilkens had spent several years in Africa, and specifically Rwanda, as a leader in providing meaningful service (e.g. building schools and coordinating social services). To what extent did this identity and experience impact not only his decision to stay but also to more actively respond to the needs of all Rwandans during the genocide?

## Chapter 10

1. What are your thoughts as you read about the couple who were in charge of the orphanage near Wilkens' home and their decision to flee Rwanda and leave behind thirty children aged 4 months to 5 years old? To what extent did the couple have an obligation to care for these children?

2. To what extent is Heri a hero? What behaviors might make him seem more heroic? What behaviors make him seem merely human? Does simply doing the right thing become heroic during genocides or other situations involving gross violations of human rights?

3. Ultimately, what do you think guided Heri's decision making?

## Chapter 11

1. As Wilkens ventured out to get his laissez pass, the first road block he encountered was operated by a tailor from his neighborhood. Wilkens notes, "He had always seemed like a nice, gentle guy, and it was strange to see him by the barrier with a weapon in his hand" (p. 62). How could a "nice, gentle" tailor have become a perpetrator of genocide? What does this scene say about the human potential for evil?

2. What was required to go through so many roadblocks to reach the Prefecture Office? What is Wilkens' thinking as he makes this journey?

3. Wilkens writes that "I didn't know it at the time, but this was the beginning of building a network of relationships, beginning with the Interahamwe on the street and going all the way up to the top leaders of the genocidal government" (p. 63). What are some possible moral dilemmas and implications of networking with the perpetrators of genocide? Is it appropriate to work with Renzaho?

## Chapter 12

1. What are your reactions to the work of the ICRC? What dilemmas does the ICRC face?

2. What kind of person would be an ICRC worker? What set of attitudes and values would be required to provide medical care during a genocide? How might the challenges of their work be different from Wilkens'?

3. By contrast, Wilkens writes about "…the festive attitude we often encountered at these barriers…to see how people could be so cold-blooded one moment and in the next moment are helping to push your car out of a ditch" (p. 68). What set of attitudes and values might the barrier guards have? What accounts for their behaviors as perpetrators?

4. What might Wilkens have been thinking and feeling as he surveyed the ADRA compound, which once had been full of resources and bustling with activity and now was empty and torn apart?

## Chapter 13

1. Wilkens finds another Seventh-day Adventist building untouched, including a working telephone. He immediately calls his parents in Spokane. What might have motivated him to do this? What might you have done if you were in a similar situation? When the call was completed, what might have been some of Wilkens' feelings?

2. As Wilkens returns home after a day full of traumatic events, he finds that those at his house and in his neighborhood have faced their own terrifying challenges as one young woman is murdered by government soldiers when she cannot find her ID. Wilkens writes, "It was so senseless – someone's life or death decided by a word written on his or her ID card. Horrible" (p. 73). What are your reactions? What words in addition to "horrible" might you use?

## Chapter 14

1. Wilkens notes that BBC reporter Mark Doyle "courageously put himself in harm's way so the rest of the world could see and hear the genocide unfold blow by blow, while it was actually happening" (p. 75).   In what ways was Doyle a hero? What roles do reporters play during wars and the atrocities that often accompany them?

2. How might Doyle's interview with Dallaire have been perceived by Westerners?

## Chapter 15

1. How easily had Wilkens' Hutu neighbor changed? Wilkens notes, "It's disturbing how putting a gun in someone's hands can change his whole personality" (p. 77). What factors might have influenced this change?

2. What is the best response to evil intentions? What choice did Wilkens make when he was told to hand over Anitha and Janvier?

3. Wilkens may have appeared powerless in this confrontation, yet he ultimately was able to deny the soldiers' demand and the workers survived. What power did Wilkens use?

## Chapter 16

1. Wilkens' describes how he began to ignore and simply accept the reality of rockets falling nearby: "…I heard the explosion, felt the deep shaking and didn't flinch, but simply continued doing what needed to be done" (p. 80). What does the acceptance of such a violent reality suggest about Wilkens and his circumstances? Can we accommodate just about any reality and keep going? Or must something be sacrificed? How is Wilkens changing?

2. Wilkens is confronted with another violent reality when Bernard (ironically a member of the Interahamwe) takes him to a courtyard full of Tutsis in horrible circumstances. To what extent are Bernard's actions surprising? How can his possible murderous actions as a member of a group committing the genocide be reconciled with his humane actions to save the Tutsis in the courtyard? What do his actions suggest about the capacity for good and evil in all people?

3. What might possibly sustain Wilkens as he responds to such brutal circumstances? How might the answer be reflected in this excerpt: "During the genocide, things that seemed so ordinary in normal times, like a mother holding her child, touched something very deep inside me and made me feel, if only for a few moments, that I was being carried away from the ugliness, pain, and brutality that sometimes threatened to drown me" (p. 84)?

4. Why might Wilkens' have reached the conclusion that it was "…best to remain an impartial humanitarian worker and not be known as someone who was only helping people with Tutsi ID cards" (p. 86)? To what extent is it possible to remain neutral?

5. What were your reactions when you found that the people living in the courtyard, including Bernard, were eventually murdered? What does Wilkens' response, "…this horrific tragedy went completely unnoticed by the rest of the world" (p. 86), suggest about his feelings?

6. In July, when the genocide came to an end, Wilkens was able to reunite the mother he had saved from the courtyard with another of her sons. What were you feeling when you read this excerpt? To what extent is this reunion a rationale, vindication, or validation of Wilkens' actions - of all the dangers and horrors he encountered? To what extent might the reunion be an affirmation of Wilkens' faith, both his faith in his Maker, and his faith in humanity?

## Chapter 17

1. What motivates Wilkens to take action after staying at home for two days because of a death threat? To what extent is this motivation similar to his original intentions for choosing to stay in Rwanda? How has his "universe of obligation" expanded as the genocide continues?

2. Again, as in the past, Wilkens finds himself involved with members of the Interahamwe to pursue a humanitarian cause. Additionally, his affiliation with Interahamwe members, related to friends in the past, allows him to transcend the death threat. Does this affiliation compromise his humanitarian goals or religious beliefs? Or do pragmatics – in this case, water for the orphans – trump everything?

3. To what extent does Wilkens' positive approach, disarming style, personal charm, and status as ADRA Director mitigate the danger?

## Chapter 18

1. While Wilkens had a compelling reason for finding larger quantities of water for the orphanages he was serving, what might have motivated the children to help Wilkens clean and fill the barrels? "Despite having to duck for cover four or five times…" (p. 93) under sniper fire, the children continued until their tasks were completed. Why did they help?

2. Wilkens suggests the children's completion of their "long, hot, dirty work" was linked to their can-do attitudes and their choice to make the task game-like. Do you agree? Were there other factors involved? Would children in other cultures (such as the US or other Western countries) have done the same thing, or was this somehow linked to the genocide and/or Rwandan culture?

## Chapter 19

1. What were some of the overwhelming dilemmas Wilkens faced if he was to rescue his ADRA colleagues in Nyamirambo? How did he begin to address what seemed like an impossible task?

2. What are your impressions of Colonel Renzaho and Major Emmanuel? To what extent were they trying to do the right thing? To what extent were they perpetrators of genocide and/or rescuers of victims? How should they be judged?

3. How difficult is it to remain hopeful in the face of such despair? What allowed Wilkens to persist in the face of a seemingly impossible situation?

4. At the end of such a harrowing day, what might be the thinking of each of the involved groups?

- Wilkens and his extended ADRA family of rescuers
- Hutu government leaders Renzaho and Emmanuel
- The Tutsi victims who were rescued

## Chapter 20

1. One day in June, as Gasigwa and Wilkens are checking on the status of the neighborhood, they come under fire. Wilkens notes that just as they are about to get back to the house, "…a bullet whizzed by me at body level. You can usually tell if they are high overhead or whistling along at body level, and this one was low" (p. 110). How does Wilkens react to the fact that someone was

apparently shooting at him? How is being the target different than witnessing random acts of violence?

2. Gasigwa was at Wilkens' side during much of the genocide. Were his motivations the same as Wilkens'? What factors might have impacted his day-to-day commitment to be a rescuer? How does his identity as a Rwandan impact his heroic acts?

3. Wilkens recalls that under similar fire, he and his neighborhood volunteers had distributed protein biscuits, which Wilkens had acquired from the UN, to children in his neighborhood. Is this bravery? Heroism? Or is it simply adaptation by ordinary people in extra-ordinary situations?

4. This chapter begins with Wilkens' account of the joy he felt connecting with his family by radio on Father's day, and ends with him cradling an orphaned infant and looking "...into her sweet face, and my heart melted instantly" (p. 113). What do these two events have in common? What do they say about how life and how human moments transcend even the most tragic of times? What do they say about Wilkens?

## Chapter 21

1. Why do you think Wilkens refused to give the baby to Angelique? How important are our "instincts" or more subjective feelings about people when we make important decisions?

2. Why do you think Tutsis sought refuge together in churches? Were they any safer there?

3. What are your reactions to Wilkens' account of the boys waiting for treatment at the Red Cross Hospital? Wilkens suggests, "It's always the kids, the ones who have no say, who pay the highest price" (p. 117). When we talk about casualties in wars, genocides, and other atrocities, do we usually think first of soldiers and other military combatants or harmless and innocent children?

4. What do you think it was like for someone without a medical background to care for Angelique's wounds? How were you feeling as you read Wilkens' narrative about changing her bandages? Which do you think was more difficult for Wilkens, repeatedly driving through the "Valley of Death" or changing the bandages?

## Chapter 22

1. Even in the midst of so much death, Wilkens finds the murder of Triphine, the Gasimba orphanage nurse, very difficult to comprehend. Why is her death especially tragic and grim for him? At some point, does facing so much death and despair reach an emotional tipping point? To what extent is resiliency possible?

2. Ironically, after killing the parents of the orphans she subsequently cared for, the Interahamwe often brought their wounded to Triphine. Wilkens asks, "How could she stand to touch their skin, to breathe the air contaminated by their stinking drunken breath? How could she bear to disinfect and bandage the wounds that these murderers sustained while committing their filthy acts" (p. 125)? What are some possible answers?

3. Wilkens writes "I want to see the way she did. I want her eyes" (p. 126). What does he mean? What does it take to see with Triphine's eyes?

## Chapter 23

1. Despite living in hellish conditions, Wilkens remains both resourceful and resilient. He sees an opportunity in a broken-down dump truck. What allows him to remain motivated and committed? What factors seem to facilitate his ability to continually solve the most challenging of problems?

**Chapter 24**

1. As he stops to pick up an empty water barrel, Wilkens is the target of machine gun fire. This has happened before. Why is it different this time? Why does he finally admit that he was shaken up by the close call? Are there only so many times someone can be placed in harm's way before becoming a victim? Is such courage limitless?

2. As he faces what appears to be an imminent slaughter of innocent women and children at the Gisimba orphanage, Carl greets the militia leader and attempts to shake his hand. He explains, "I know it sounds ridiculous to ask this guy for help when he is the one commanding these killers. He was most likely the mastermind behind the massacre planned for that night. But I acted toward him as I had toward so many other vicious people during the genocide. I tried to approach and treat him like a decent, respectable person. That was my strategy for improving the chances of getting a decent and respectable response" (p. 134). To what extent was this a good strategy? How had this approach worked previously for Wilkens? Why might working with perpetrators in a "decent and respectable" manner be troubling to some?

3. What made Wilkens' decision to leave the orphanage to look for help so agonizing? Why did he call it "…one of the hardest decisions I had made during the whole genocide" (p. 137)?

4. In one of the most important scenes of the book, Wilkens confronts Prime Minister Jean Kambanda and asks for his help to stop the impending massacre at the orphanage. To Wilkens' surprise, Kambanda, one of the primary orchestrators of the genocide, agrees to help and immediately tells his subordinates to take action. After the Genocide, Kambanda was convicted of committing genocide and crimes against humanity by the International Criminal Court (ICC) and sentenced to life in prison.

What makes judging Kambanda's actions, as well as Wilkens' decision to work with perpetrators, so difficult to interpret? How could Kambanda rescue some but massacre others? Other Hutus who worked with Wilkens were charged with committing genocide and they asked for Wilkens' help when they faced imprisonment. Did he have the obligation to help them?

5. Regardless of the outcome, did Wilkens make the right decision to go home rather than return to the Gasimba Orphanage? Why might he have made this decision? Was it consistent with his previous actions?

## Chapter 25

1. To what extent did Wilkens rely on the UN? In what ways would working with a larger institution such as the UN have benefited Wilkens? For instance, might he have felt safer? Or conversely, was there a downside to being affiliated with the UN? Was Wilkens able to accomplish more as a single individual? What might his experiences teach us about the multiple roles of governments, NGOs, and the acts of individuals and their power to make changes?

2. At the end of the genocide, General Dallaire of the UN asks Wilkens, "How the hell did you do what you did?" Wilkens responds: "…we did what we did one day at a time…" (p. 146). What does Wilkens mean? What does his response suggest about individual heroic acts and how heroes develop?

## Chapter 26

1. Wilkens notes his surprise when he saw a Catholic priest (Father Wenceslas Munyeshyaka) at Holy Family Church with a pistol shoved in his belt. What does Wilkens' reaction say about his instincts? What is your reaction to the fact that this priest later was convicted of involvement in the genocide for delivering hundreds

of adults and children to the Interahamwe and other militias who brutally murdered them? What must have the victims been thinking and feeling as they sought refuge in churches, only to be betrayed?

2. Discuss the tremendous irony between the actions of the five Catholic Sisters of Charity who protected orphans (see pages 54 & 55) and Father Munyeskyaka. What does it say about the potential for good and evil in all people, regardless of roles and expectations? What does it say about making generalizations about social institutions, including churches, religion, and religious workers? Are some actions and some perpetrators more evil and immoral than others?

3. When he returned to collect the orphans' clothing and blankets, what was Wilkens thinking as he found himself facing the Interahamwe killing gang as they looted the Gisimba orphanage? Likewise, when he was forced into the green Mercedes to get the additional truck, what was going through Wilkens' mind? To what extent were you fearful for him as you read these sections?

4. What does Wilkens believe "transformed" the Interahamwe members from perpetrators to helpers? What do their actions say about the nature of goodness, evil, and being human? Are people either good or evil, or are people neutral and capable of acting either way? How else might people be transformed?

## Chapter 27

1. What do you think about Wilkens' willingness to go about his work under sniper fire? To what extent has the danger become normal and mundane? Does that make the situation more dangerous?

2. What are your feelings as you read the section about the little boy from the sniper attack as he is examined by Wilkens? When

children cry or complain and no obvious cause can be found, what assumptions are made? In this case, what must have been going through Wilkens' mind as he saw the entry wound and later the bullet just beneath the skin?

3. To what extent was Wilkens' interaction with the Interahamwe teenager the most dangerous encounter yet? What actions by Wilkens suggest he also sensed the danger?

4. Was it random luck, simply fate, or the residue of Wilkens' good acts that lead to the connections among the father, his wounded son, Wilkens, and the teenager with the weapon, as well as the eventual peaceful resolution of a tense encounter?

## Chapter 28

1. What must have been Wilkens' thinking as he and the rest of his household waited inside as the Tutsi soldiers of the RPF took over their neighborhood? Why might there have been considerable fear and trepidation? While Wilkens had learned to deal with the Hutu perpetrators, would dealing with the RPF necessarily mean peace and greater security?

2. What compels Wilkens to act when Janvier is questioned in a threatening manner?

3. As the RPF soldiers look over the orphanage, Wilkens describes how proud he was of Heri's "…determination, compassion, and bravery" to care for the orphans during the genocide. What other words might be used to describe Wilkens' work?

4. Who was responsible for ending the genocide? What are Wilkens' obvious feelings toward the RPF?

5. What does Wilkens think when he hears about Angelique's actual identity? To what extent is there some sense of irony or justice about her death? Again, did Wilkens' good deeds have an

unintended or unanticipated impact?

6. After 88 days of hellish experience, what was it like for Wilkens to re-enter a more normal existence?

## **NOTE: there are additional chapter questions for discussion prepared by high school seniors at** http://www.imnotleavingrwanda.com/ We encourage you to add questions to the website!

# *I'm Not Leaving* - **Educator's Guide**

"I'm not Leaving," is a book and an accompanying film account of the 1994 Rwandan genocide against the Tutsi through the eyes of Carl Wilkens, the only known American aid worker who remained in Rwanda. The history of the genocide in Rwanda in 1994 is a difficult story of paralysis and injustice. Almost the entire world stood by as nearly a million men, women and children were murdered. But it also is a story of a few who refused to stand by as the atrocity unfolded. It is a story of choosing to be an "upstander" rather than a bystander, to rescue, and to act upon one's beliefs. It is a story of courage, survival, and the decision to say, "I'm not leaving."

"It still looked like there was no end in sight. The fear was so real, especially the first few days. You didn't want to die. You love your wife. You love your kids. You want to be reunited with them. But when you make the right choice, and taking action – doing something – you know there is a reason to be on earth. And you know that the whole world just hasn't gone crazy, as it looked like here."

-Carl Wilkens

## <u>Rationale</u>

*I'm Not Leaving* provides students with an opportunity to study a difficult history that has the potential to transform their understanding of themselves and the world. Some historical narratives are celebratory and reinforce the power of nationalism and other forces of the dominant ideology. By contrast, some narratives are more emotive and controversial, and remind us that the study of history becomes more meaningful as we consider multiple narratives.

If people are to actively participate in a free democracy, Margot

Stern Strom, Director of Facing History and Ourselves, argues that we must educate students, "to value their rights as citizens and take responsibility for their actions. To do so, they must know not only the triumphs of history but also the failures, the tragedies, and the humiliations."

* Becoming a more informed citizen and critical thinker involves examining multiple perspectives, including the tragedies of history, not just the triumphs.  This critical examination can lead to a greater understanding of the challenges of our modern world, but more importantly, critical comprehension can become the basis for informed and just action.

Strom notes, "If we are to win the struggle for the nation's conscience and future, we must counter lessons of hate with lessons that promote understanding and caring. We must help students examine their thoughts and feelings and then confront not only their own potential for passivity and complicity but also their courage and resilience. And we must teach them to value their rights as citizens and take responsibility for their actions." She also warns that "…unless students are encouraged to make moral judgments, they are likely to become paralyzed by their own thinking and therefore unable to respond to injustice" (p. xxii of *Holocaust and Human Behavior*).

## Excerpts from the California *"Model Curriculum for Human Rights and Genocide"*

There is no more urgent task for educators in the field of history and social science than to teach students about the importance of human rights and to analyze with them the actual instances in which genocide – the ultimate violation of human rights – has been committed. We study the atrocities of the past not only to preserve their significance as historical events but also to help identify ways to prevent the atrocities from ever happening again.

The study of human rights and genocide requires intellectual honesty and moral courage, for no nation or society in human history has been totally innocent of human rights abuses. It is necessary to acknowledge unflinchingly the instances in United States history when our own best ideals were betrayed by the systematic mistreatment of group members because of their race, religion, culture, language, gender, or political views. When studying other societies, we must be equally candid. Whether historical or contemporary, human rights abuses must be acknowledged, and students must learn that individuals and groups have been tortured, murdered, confined to psychiatric hospitals, or subjected to discriminatory treatment because of their race, religion, culture, gender, political views, or other personal characteristics that make them "different."

## Possible Themes

- We/They
- Choices, Conformity, and Obedience
- Perpetrators and Victims,
- Upstanders and Bystanders

# Prior to Viewing the Film and/or Reading the Book Lesson Plan/Activities

### Lesson 1: What do we know about genocides?

(more info in PDF's at http://www.imnotleavingrwanda.com/)

1. Use the "genocide wall" activity to access participant/student's current knowledge of the term.

2. After participants/students have completed their individual and group activities, have them complete a quick-write summary and reflection. What have they learned and what is the significance of it?

3. Pass out a world map and ask participants/students to identify places where genocides of the past 100 years have occurred. Participants/students may work individually or in smaller groups on this. Once they have identified genocide sites, share the map "Genocidal Acts of the Twentieth Century*." Have participants/students note which genocides they identified and those they missed.

*This map is taken from the unit "Confronting Genocide: Never Again?" from the Choices program at Brown University. The unit is available at http://www.choices.edu.

**Lesson 2: What is a genocide?** (more info in PDF's at http://www.imnotleavingrwanda.com/)

1. Introduce the "found poem" approach.

2. Ask participants/students to use content from the "United Nations Convention on the Prevention and Punishment of the Crime of Genocide" to write a found poem. Participants/students can work individually or in smaller groups to write and share their poems. Use a quick-write to identify key elements and patterns.

# Acknowledgments

So many people have helped that I'm sure I'm going to leave someone out. In any case, I do know where I want to start.

First, many thanks to Teresa, Mindy, Lisa, Shaun, Mom, and Dad for your constant encouragement and endless readings of drafts. Your feedback was always the most helpful. Teresa and Mindy: I don't want to count how many times you have worked through the night—thank you!

Thanks to friends and other family members who gave editorial help along the way. Thanks, Helen Kweskin, for early editorial help and affirming feedback when I felt so unsure and really needed it. Thanks, Brooke Schlange: your red comments were always welcome. Thanks, Noah Bopp, Ryan and Nicole Moore, Andrew Finstuen, and Cindy Magi, for your candid feedback. As I said, there are many of you, and I still haven't listed all who took time to read and respond to drafts. A special thanks to Dr. James D. Brown for generously giving so much of his time in preparing the Analysis/Discussion and Educators guides.

Thanks to my Rwandan friends who are mentioned in these pages . . . I can't begin to express the feelings of gratitude and respect that I hold for you! I'm tempted to start mentioning specific names here, but I will contain myself and save up for later. I hope you will all read of my love and respect for you in the stories.

Thanks, Carl

# About Carl Wilkens

As a humanitarian aid worker with the Adventist Church, Carl Wilkens moved his young family to Rwanda in the spring of 1990. When the genocide was launched in April 1994, Wilkens refused to leave, even when urged to do so by close friends, his church, and the United States government. He was the only American to remain in Kigali throughout the genocide, though thousands of expatriates evacuated, and the United Nations pulled out most of their troops. Venturing out each day into streets crackling with mortars and gunfire, Wilkens worked his way through roadblocks of angry, bloodstained soldiers and civilians armed with machetes and assault rifles in order to bring food, water, and medicines to groups of orphans trapped around the city. His actions saved the lives of hundreds of people.

Carl and his wife, Teresa, have founded an educational nonprofit called World Outside My Shoes. Traveling full-time around the world, they are telling stories from Rwanda and inviting people to enter the world of the "other." They believe that stories and service are two of the most powerful tools that every person possesses to build peace.

To learn more about their work, please visit them on the web at:
http://worldoutsidemyshoes.org/
or
Facebook: World Outside My Shoes

To schedule a presentation in your area or
for any other questions, please email:
contactwoms@gmail.com

The Wilkens Family

To learn more about their work, please visit them on the web at:
http://worldoutsidemyshoes.org/
or
Facebook: World Outside My Shoes

To schedule a presentation in your area or
for any other questions, please email:
contactwoms@gmail.com